W9-BGF-516

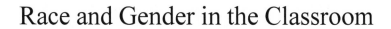

Race and Gender in the Classroom

Race and Gender in the Classroom

Teachers, Privilege, and Enduring Social Inequalities

Laurie Cooper Stoll

LEXINGTON BOOKS
Lanham • Boulder • New York • Toronto • Plymouth, UK

Published by Lexington Books
A wholly owned subsidiary of The Rowman & Littlefield Publishing Group, Inc.
4501 Forbes Boulevard, Suite 200, Lanham, Maryland 20706
www.rowman.com

10 Thornbury Road, Plymouth PL6 7PP, United Kingdom

British Library Cataloguing in Publication Information Available

Library of Congress Cataloging-in-Publication Data

Stoll, Laurie Cooper.
Race and gender in the classroom : teachers, privilege, and enduring social inequalities / Laurie
Cooper Stoll.
pages cm.
Includes bibliographical references and index.
ISBN 978-0-7391-7642-9 (cloth : alk. paper) -- ISBN 978-0-7391-7643-6 (electronic)
1. Critical pedagogy--United States. 2. Education--Social aspects--United States. 3. Feminism and
education--United States. 4. Racism in education--United States. 5. Educational equalization--Unied
States. I. Title.
LC196.5.U6S86 2013
370.11'5--dc23
2013012583

∞™ The paper used in this publication meets the minimum requirements of American
National Standard for Information Sciences Permanence of Paper for Printed Library
Materials, ANSI/NISO Z39.48-1992.

Printed in the United States of America

For Cory

Contents

Acknowledgments

In many ways this project was a labor of love, and I am very grateful for those who have nurtured it and nurtured me along the way. First, I would like to thank Judy Wittner, David Embrick, and Jennifer Parks for their mentorship while I was a doctoral student at Loyola University Chicago. A special thanks goes to David Embrick, who wrote the foreword for this book. Thank you, Dave, for always being there to lend an ear, offer advice, and push me to challenge myself in new ways. You have always been an ally.

In addition, I would like to thank the Schmitt Foundation for awarding me a generous fellowship to complete this work. As a Schmitt Dissertation Fellow, I was able to devote my full attention and energies during the 2010-2011 academic year to this research for which I am most grateful. Further, this project would not have come to fruition had it not been for the wonderful teachers who so graciously volunteered their time and welcomed me into their classrooms.

I am also very fortunate to have a number of extremely strong women in my life who serve as shining examples of perseverance and determination, particularly my mother, Tammy Norman, my grandmother, Jean Cooper, and my sister and closest friend, Amber Swain. I would not be where I am today if it were not for your unconditional love and support. I would also like to thank Crystal Jackson and Kelly Pinter for your friendship over the years, and for your patience with me as I monopolized many of our conversations over coffee with talk of this research. I love and adore you both. I owe a special debt of gratitude to my very dear friend, Erika Anderson, who on more occasions than I can remember sat and chatted with me about this book. What a joy to have you to bounce ideas off of, think through challenges in the classroom, and theorize about how to make our schools a better place for our children and for all children.

I am also appreciative of the warm welcome I received as an Assistant Professor in the Sociology and Archaeology Department at the University of Wisconsin-La Crosse. In particular, the kindness and support from Enilda Delgado, Carol Miller, Kim Vogt, and Christine Hippert helped sustain me through the final stages of this book and through my first year in La Crosse. I would also like to thank my team at Lexington, led by Jana Hodges-Kluck, for their guidance throughout the production process.

I would also be remiss if I did not acknowledge the wonderful students I have had the pleasure to work with over the past eleven years. In particular, I would like to thank Kat Klima who at the time this book goes to press will be starting her career as a classroom teacher working with students in a Title I school in Florida. Kat, I enjoyed every minute we spent talking about the challenges in this book, our shared concerns about social inequalities, and how to make the world a better place. When I advocate for more feminist, antiracist teachers in the classroom, you are whom I envision.

Last, but never least, I would like to thank my husband, Chuck, and my daughters, Emily and Anna, who have been with me on this journey every step of the way. Chuck, if I have learned anything over the past nineteen years, it's that it is possible to fall in love with the same person over and over again. Thank you for always supporting me and loving me at my worst. To Emily and Anna, the two of you are the ultimate motivation for the work I do. You keep me grounded, and I love you both more than either of you could ever imagine.

Foreword

The Hidden Curriculum: Color-blind Racism and Gender-blind Sexism in the Classroom

David G. Embrick

Civil Rights activist and sociologist W.E.B. Du Bois eloquently remarked in his 1903 book, *Souls of Black Folk,* that the problem of the Twentieth Century would be the problem of the color-line.[1] Equally inspiring for a young scholar of his time, Du Bois noted that the rights of women and the rights of African Americans were intertwined.[2] Indeed, he claimed that the rights of women needed addressing before the rights of African Americans could truly be attended. Du Bois was certainly ahead of his time in his understanding of the race, class, and gender issues of the day, and he was definitely a prognosticator when it came to understanding how race (but also class and gender) would play out in the Twentieth Century. But what can we predict beyond the twentieth century? As other social scientists have pointed out and as Professor Cooper Stoll so astutely notes in the first chapter of this book, one could easily argue that we could, and should, extend Du Bois' predictions of the problem of the color-line (and gender-line) to the Twenty-First Century.

In spite of all the progress that has been made in the past 50 years, race and gender continue to matter in the lives of women and minorities. Where it matters and how it matters for these groups, however, depends on where one lives; how one was socialized; and one's access to economic, social, political, and cultural capital. Regardless, the bottom line is that race and gender are very important social topics in all of our lives and perhaps no institution is more adept at reproducing racial and gender inequality than the U.S. educational system. Consider the following facts:

- According to the Schott Report,[3] only 47% of Black male students graduate from high school, as opposed to 78% of their White male counterparts. Further, Black male students are the least likely to graduate from high school in 33 of 48 states. Equally disturbing, the rate of the school-to-prison pipeline for young Black men exceeds the rate of high school graduation.
- According to 2010-2011 data from the Department of Education, large racial achievement gaps at the high school level continue to exist between Blacks, Latino/as, and Native Americans and their White and Asian counterparts.[4]
- Students coming from under-resourced schools are often disadvantaged in higher education (even if they are at the top of their class) because many such schools are more focused on producing workers, rather than college students.
- There is a growing gender gap at all education levels with girls scoring higher than boys on reading and writing exams, and girls and women outnumbering boys and men in attendance of honors courses and in enrollment in colleges and universities; the gender gap is even more pronounced among Latino/as and Blacks.[5]
- In spite of the gender gap, girls continue to receive an unequal education in our nation's schools; moreover, girls learn through what Peggy Orenstein calls the "hidden curriculum" that their place in society is in the softer sciences and that they are basically subservient to their male counterparts when it comes to their location in the social hierarchy.[6]

These patterns of racial and gender disparities do not stop with the high school years. In fact, there is overwhelming data that suggests these disparities continue through college, although the reasons for the disparities vary depending on race, class, immigration status, and other social factors. For example, according to the PEW Hispanic Center, Latino/as are second to Asians in attendance at colleges and universities. Yet, graduation rates remain low due in part to concentration in two-year colleges, part-time enrollment, and a tendency to go to college later in life.[7] Nonetheless, similar to high school graduation rates, Black and Latino/a students face alarming statistics when it comes to higher education. Consider these additional facts:

- According to the Education Sector Reports, Black students starting college at the beginning of the millennium were 2 and a half times more likely to enroll at a school with a 70 percent chance of NOT graduating within six years than a school with a 70 percent chance of earning a degree. Thus, fewer than half of the Black students who enroll in college graduate from four-year institutions within six years.

- According to a recent article titled "Missed Opportunities," first-generation students are less likely to complete the necessary steps to enroll in a four-year institution. In addition, first-generation students are far less likely to aspire to a bachelor's degree or higher, take the SAT or ACT exams or even apply to a four-year institution in comparison to students with at least one parent who has a bachelor's degree.
- Even though girls today outperform their male counterparts when it comes to high school graduation rates (74% of female students graduate high school compared to 67% of male students) and have pulled even with boys in math and science achievement, they face gender bias in college admissions with some highly selective colleges admitting one-third less female applicants than male applicants. [8]

The facts I have outlined above only scratch the surface when it comes to understanding white privilege and male privilege in the U.S. education system. From K-12 and into higher education, women and minorities face ongoing challenges in the classroom. These challenges range from access to adequate resources and safe learning environments to color-blind and gender-blind racial and sexist practices by teachers, administrators, classroom peers, and parents.

THE NEED FOR THIS RESEARCH!

Academic research on racial and gender bias and discrimination in education can be murky at times. There is a tendency to place blame on individual actors such as teachers, administrators, parents or even students for failures in the U.S. educational system. Other times, the school systems are criticized for being ineffective or uncaring. Less research can be found addressing larger structural issues of inequality—that is, how systemic racism and sexism create and maintain racial and gender inequity in our society. Indeed, according to critical race and education scholars Mark Chesler, Amanda Lewis, and James Crowfoot, much of social science research is premised on prejudice as opposed to structural racism (and sexism). [9] Within the field of sociology there are major differences between scholars who place primacy on teachers or families as opposed to the educational institution or larger notions of how racial and gender ideologies fundamentally shape how we think and approach secondary, primary, or higher education. For example, scholars such as Irenee Beattie argue that in order to understand some of the existing racial and gender inequalities in education, one must take a firm look at not just a student's experience in school but also the parenting style of that student. Other scholars such as Amanda Lewis and Barrie Thorne have long argued that schools are essentially race- and gender-making institutions. For them, it is true that families and parenting style matter. But schools are incubators for existing racial and gender stereotypes. From a very early age students are labeled by race and gender and socialized into understanding their identities and others' through those gendered and racialized lenses. Of course, as Eduardo Bonilla-Silva, Susan J. Douglas, Charles Gallagher, Joe R. Feagin, Nijole V. Benokraitis and other critical race and gender scholars have noted, such education struggles reflect the contests that take place within the larger community—and understanding how race, racism, gender and sexism work in higher education is inseparable from understanding how race, racism, gender, and sexism operate in our larger society.

Enter Laurie Cooper Stoll's book, *Race and Gender in the Classroom*, a thought-provoking, carefully woven examination of color-blind racism and gender-blind sexism in the twenty-first century classroom. Cooper Stoll argues that contrary to the commonsense notion that education is a great equalizer when it comes to social mobility for any group, and despite what most folks in our society today believe about race and gender—that we are post-racial and post-gendered and that racism and sexism have become issues of the past—our current educational climate is one that is complex and often "paradoxical." Cooper Stoll argues that well-intentioned teachers often rely on color-blind and gender-blind frames to help navigate and understand race- and gender-related issues both inside and outside of the classroom. The end result is a wonderful ethnographic account of the lives of 18 teachers in three school settings in Chicago over an academic year. Her observations in the classroom and in interactions with the teachers give insight to the challenges these teachers face as they struggle with the school system and with trying to understand the racial and gender matters they are confronted with throughout the school year. More importantly, this study provides an in-depth examination of how race and gender continue to operate in an institution and society that purports to be post-racial and post-gendered. In such a context, well-intentioned race- and gender-neutral policies, for example, end up creating racialized and gendered outcomes that ultimately affect students' lives. In that regard, I am reminded of Lelant T. Saito's 2009 book, *The Politics of Exclusion: The Failure of Race-Neutral Policies in Urban America*.[10] In this book, Saito argues that many contemporary "race-neutral" policies, even those put into place by folks who believe they are working to free society of racial discrimination, may in fact produce racialized outcomes. Thus, individual efforts (i.e., policies) that operate in a context of systemic racism and sexism, no matter how sincere they are, tend to reproduce the status quo of inequality. Cooper Stoll suggests this may be no different when it comes to understanding policy outcomes in our educational system.

In this well-organized and researched book, Cooper Stoll provides us with a deeper understanding of the lives of schoolteachers who have to carefully balance their worldview of race and gender with the worldview (and experiences) of race and gender their students face. What we, as readers, end up with is a rare look at the hidden mechanisms of color-blind racism and gender-blind sexism within a particular institutional setting. And we are asked to reassess how we might go about addressing continued racial and gender disparities when we are faced with the prospect that we must do more than engage in policies that ultimately maintain the status quo or produce racialized and gendered outcomes. But, before we can truly begin to have serious dialogue about what progressive changes we need to have in our educational system and how we might go about creating and implementing these changes, we must first acknowledge the systemic and institutional nature of race and gender in our schools. Luckily for us, Cooper Stoll's research continues where other critical scholars have left off and provides us with the insight needed to make real changes for the better.

David G. Embrick
Loyola University-Chicago

NOTES

1. Du Bois, W.E.B. 1903. *Souls of Black Folks.* New York, NY: Penguin Books.
2. For a deeper analysis of W.E.B. Du Bois' conceptualization of race, class, and gender, see: Hattery, Angela J., and Earl Smith. 2005. "William Edward Burghardt Du Bois and the Concepts of Race, Class and Gender." *Sociation Today*, Vol. 3 (1).
3. For a full review of the Schott report, see: "The Schott 50 State Report on Public Education and Black Males 2010." *Schott Foundation for Higher Education.*
4. For more insight to these facts, see: Nhan, Doris. 2012. "Interactive: State High School Graduation Rates by Race, Ethnicity." *National Journal: The Next America.* http://www.nationaljournal.com/thenextamerica/education/interactive-state-high-school-graduation-rates-by-race-ethnicity-20121130 .
5. For more on the this topic, see: Lopez, Nancy. 2003. *Hopeful Girls, Troubled Boys: Race and Gender Disparity in Urban Education.* New York, NY: Routledge.
6. See Orenstein, Peggy. 1994. *School Girls: Young Women, Self-Esteem, and the Confidence Gap.* New York, NY: Anchor Books.
7. See Lopez, Mark Hugo. 2009. "Latinos and Education: Explaining the Attainment Gap." *Pew Research Hispanic Center.* http://www.pewhispanic.org/2009/10/07/latinos-and-education-explaining-the-attainment-gap/ .
8. C2 Education. 2012. "The Gender Inequality Pendulum." http://www.c2educate.com/blog-2/the-gender-inequality-pendulum/ .
9. Chesler, Mark, Amanda Lewis, and James Crowfoot. 2005. *Challenging Racism in Higher Education: Promoting Justice.* Lanham, MD: Roman & Littlefield Publishers, Inc.
10. Saito, Leland T. 2009. *The Politics of Exclusion: The Failure of Race-Neutral Policies in Urban America.* Stanford, CA: Stanford University Press.

Chapter One

Constructing the Color- and Gender-Blind Classroom

It was a cold, gray day in November when I drove to Morgan Elementary, a predominantly white school just north of Chicago, for another day of observing teachers and students in classrooms. On that particular day, I was doing my second observation of Mr. Gold's third grade general education class. Mr. Gold was one of four teachers in this study, interestingly all men, who came to teaching later in life as a second career. I arrived in Mr. Gold's classroom shortly after 9:00 o'clock and found the students working independently at their desks. They had just finished reading a short story about a boy who worked a paper route (something most of the students admitted they had never heard of) and were answering questions about it on a worksheet Mr. Gold had given them.

One of the things I immediately noticed about the exercise was that it was designed to challenge the students to think critically, not just test basic reading comprehension like most of the exercises I had observed teachers using. When I mentioned this to Mr. Gold he told me he either created these exercises himself or sought them out from other educational sources. However, according to Mr. Gold, the principal at Morgan "would not be happy" if he were to come into the classroom and see him deviating from the standard curriculum. As Mr. Gold told me, "They want everything cookie cutter now."

After the students turned in their worksheets, he instructed them to come to the carpet. As the students gathered on the rug in front of the classroom with their legs "crisscross applesauce" ready for the morning's read-aloud, I noticed three white girls sitting behind the only Black girl in the class, Rachel, tentatively reaching their hands out as they contemplated touching her hair. The look on their faces was one of curiosity as if Rachel's hair was

1

somehow strange and exotic and they were interested to know how it might feel in their fingers but were hesitant to find out. Rachel, with her back to the girls, was oblivious to what was going on behind her.

Meanwhile, Mr. Gold pulled a book of Aesop's fables from his bookshelf and informed the students that someone was coming to their class in a couple of weeks to help them make puppets. The puppet exercise, according to Mr. Gold, was directly related to their lesson this week on fables. He then began by reading the classic fable, *The Tortoise and the Hare*. Afterward, he asked the students if they could identify the moral of the story. Several students immediately shouted out without raising their hands:

"Even if you're slow, you can still win."

"You're not always fastest."

"If you're good at something, don't brag about it."

"Don't brag about it, be humble or everyone will hate you."

Mr. Gold chimed in, "Don't take things for granted."

He then launched into a second fable, *The Fox and the Goat.* Unlike in *The Tortoise and the Hare*, however, this time the "underdog" did not come out on top. In fact, the cunning fox outsmarted the unsuspecting goat to free himself from the well he was trapped in leaving the goat trapped instead. Mr. Gold looked visibly surprised by this ending, perhaps because he had just finished *The Tortoise and the Hare* where the slow, but determined tortoise wins the race in the end. He closed the book, looked to me to see my reaction, shrugged his shoulders, and then begrudgingly admitted to his students, "Sometimes the weak do not win." Indeed. So why did Mr. Gold appear hesitant to concede this reality to his students? As I will argue in this book, Mr. Gold's reluctance to acknowledge that life is not fair, that inequality *does* exist, is a direct reflection of the construction of color- and gender-blind classrooms in an era of "post-racial" and "post-gendered" politics.

COLOR-BLIND RACISM AND GENDER-BLIND SEXISM IN THE TWENTY-FIRST CENTURY

In 1903, W.E.B. Du Bois wrote, "The problem of the Twentieth Century is the problem of the color-line." (34) Given the racial disparities that continue to exist in schooling in the United States, it seems clear the problem of the color-line Du Bois wrote of persists in the twenty-first century. Yet, how to conceptualize and measure racial discrimination has often proven as controversial as how to categorize race. If one takes into account responses to typical survey measures used to assess prejudicial attitudes in the U.S. it would appear Americans are becoming more racially tolerant. Overall, opposition to busing, residential segregation, and even interracial marriage has decreased substantially when compared with survey responses thirty years ago (Davis, Smith and Marsden 2002). Other methodological approaches, however, have yielded data that paint a very different picture of race relations in the U.S. For example, while opposition to interracial marriage measured by survey data has precipitously decreased, when respondents are questioned using in-depth interviews if they would marry someone of a different race or approve of their children marrying someone of a different race, the responses are overwhelmingly negative (Bonilla-Silva 2006).

According to Eduardo Bonilla-Silva (1997), the new form of racism that exists in the United States in the post-Civil Rights era is "color-blind." Color-blind racism (Bonilla-Silva 2006) manifests in four basic frames used predominantly by whites to interpret information about race: abstract liberalism, naturalization, cultural racism, and minimization of racism. Abstract liberalism relies on the basic principles of political and economic liberalism to explain racial matters, for example, the justification of whites' opposition to forced integration based on the liberal belief that all individuals should have a "choice" of where they want to live (2006: 28). The naturalization frame explains racial phenomena in terms of natural occurrences; for instance, the choice to date only partners of the same race is not due to racism, but the belief that people are "naturally" attracted to others of the same race. Cultural racism relies on culturally based arguments to explain racial inequality such as the belief that Black children perform poorly in school because the "Black culture" does not value education. Finally, minimization of racism is based on the notion that discrimination is no longer a major determinate of life chances for racial minorities; therefore, what appear to be racialized outcomes can be explained away by factors other than racism (2006: 29).

According to Bonilla-Silva (2006), "The central component of any dominant racial ideology is its frames or *set paths for interpreting information.*" (26; emphasis in original) In essence, the frames of color-blind racism operate like cul-de-sacs because "after people filter issues through them, they explain racial phenomena following a predictable route." (26) Feminist theorists have long argued as much about dominant gender ideologies and the ways in which they influence how people interpret information about gender and perform gender in everyday life (e.g., Connell 1987; West and Fenstermaker 1987; Butler 1990; Bem 1993; Lorber 1994; Risman 1999; Collins 2000; Johnson 2005).

Like color-blind racism in the post-Civil Rights era, contemporary "gender-blind sexism" operates in a culture in which blatant sexism is *supposedly* rejected yet sexist ideologies, policies, and practices continue. This "modern

sexism" as Nijole Benokraitis and Joe Feagin referred to it in1986, is predicated on the assumption that because society is now "post-gendered," what
sexism remains resides only in *individual* acts of prejudice or discrimination
on the part of sexist persons who are out of touch with mainstream beliefs
about gender. In Benokraitis and Feagin's work, they further distinguished
this type of modern sexism as subtle sex discrimination and covert sex discrimination. Whereas subtle sex discrimination refers to the unequal, harmful
treatment of women that is visible but goes unacknowledged because of the
internalization of sexist behaviors, covert sex discrimination refers to the
unequal, harmful treatment of women that is hidden and maliciously moti-
vated (30-31). According to Benokraitis and Feagin, although covert sex
discrimination is difficult to prove, subtle sex discrimination is even more so
because it is generally accepted as "normal" behavior, not discrimination.

I argue that within the present "post-racial" and "post-gendered" era of
assumed social equality, individuals' generally interpret information about
gender much like race through the frames of abstract liberalism, naturalization, cultural "sexism," and the minimization of "sexism." For example, at
the most fundamental level, abstract liberalism asserts that no demographic
group should be singled out for special treatment; instead, every American
should have access to equal opportunities or have autonomous choice in
matters of residence or access to resources (Bonilla-Silva 2006). When it
comes to race, whites tend to use abstract liberalism to explain their opposition to policies intended to address racial inequalities such as affirmative
action if in fact such policies are viewed as "privileging" certain (non-white)
groups over other (white) groups. When it comes to gender, individuals tend
to rely on abstract liberalism to reject policies such as the Lilly Ledbetter Act
or a woman's right to choose, if such initiatives are seen as benefitting or
impinging upon the rights of one particular gender over another. Like racial
equality, gender equality is assumed to be a zero sum game.

From a naturalization perspective (Bonilla-Silva 2006), segregation is not
the result of racism but "biological" or "natural" phenomena; the reason that
individuals tend to self-segregate is not because they are socialized to identify primarily with their racial group but because "like attracts like." Obviously, there is also widespread appeal for using this same logic when it
comes to gender, although in the case of gender (as opposed to race present-
ly) there tends to be far less stigma for privileging biological explanations of
social differences. The common wisdom is that while socialization may account for some differences between boys and girls, they are essentially hardwired differently (e.g., Sax 2005).

Further, just as cultural racism relies on culturally based arguments to
explain racial differences, *cultural sexism* relies on culturally based arguments to explain gender differences. The same logic used to buttress claims
about gender and sexism using the naturalization framework is still present,

but unlike naturalization that views these differences as the outgrowth of organic or biological processes, cultural sexism views differences as the result of social processes that distinguish certain types of men and women. Within this frame deviation from traditional gender role socialization based on hegemonic masculinity, emphasized femininity, and homophobia (Connell 1987) is generally called upon to justify the unequal station of boys and girls and women and men in the larger society, as well as the unequal station of those who are straight and those who are gay, lesbian, or bisexual, for example.

Finally, minimization of racism seeks to explain away current racial disparities, if they are acknowledged at all, as the result of factors that have nothing to do with racial discrimination. According to Bonilla-Silva (2006), minimization of racism is evident in statements such as "It's better now than in the past," or "There is discrimination, but there are plenty of jobs out there." (29) Similarly, minimization of sexism uses the same logic when it comes to gender: gender inequality either does not exist at present, or if it does exist it is due to reasons other than modern-day sexism. For example, the reason that women are more likely to major in psychology as opposed to engineering is not because women are tracked out of engineering fields or because women tend to be marginalized if they do enter them (Bobbit-Zeher 2007; Colander and Holmes 2007); it is because women are just not as *good* as men at math and science. Note that, much like with race, individuals often rely on any combination of gender-blind frames to explain why this is the case: (1) women and men have the same educational opportunities today, women simply do not *choose* to go into male-dominated fields (abstract liberalism); (2) women, unlike men, do not have the spatial skills required to go into math and science fields (naturalization); and/or (3) women prefer fields like psychology as opposed to engineering because they are more interested in building relationships than building cities (cultural sexism).

Taken together, the frames of color-blind racism and gender-blind sexism reflect "commonsense" notions about race and gender that are used to justify contemporary racial and gender inequality (Bonilla-Silva 2006). As Bonilla-Silva argues, if the ultimate goal of the dominant race is to maintain their position of privilege within a racialized society, they must develop rationalizations to account for the status of minorities (9). This is also true with patriarchy; to maintain power, authority, and privilege, men must develop rationalizations to account for the status of women and men of subordinated masculinities (Connell 1987). In other words, how do dominant group members explain racial and gender inequality in a "post-racial" and "post-gendered" society?

My research finds that teachers rely on various frames of color-blind racism and gender-blind sexism as they struggle to understand and explain race- and gender-related issues in the classroom and beyond. Yet, while it is important to hold teachers accountable anytime they perpetuate prejudice or discrimination, this book is not about laying the blame for racial and gender inequality at the feet of teachers. As I argue, teachers' attitudes must be understood within a particular institutional context that provides them no incentive for acknowledging, let alone addressing institutional racism or sexism. In the following chapters, I will show how teachers carry out their professional roles in a very complex system of ruling relations (Smith 1990; 2005) rooted in color-blind and gender-blind ideologies. These ideologies are best reflected in the adoption of what I refer to as the *social equality maxim*. The social equality maxim is the belief that all students have the potential to be successful regardless of social location. In other words, race and gender do not matter; neither have the ability to limit a student's capacity to flourish in the classroom or in life.

The social equality maxim is fundamentally manifest in the construction of what I define as *color-* and *gender-blind classrooms*: learning environments where all students have the same opportunities for success; all children are equally loved and valued; and the problems of race, gender, and other contentious identities are illusory. As Mr. Gira, a fifth grade teacher at Morgan Elementary told me, "I've just found that I try not to see gender, you know, race, that stuff—you just can't even look at that. They're [students] just people. I think that's the smartest way to approach it." Of course, the color- and gender-blind classroom exists more in theory than in practice, as it is rife with paradox. For example, while intersectionality scholars challenge us to take account of the ways that systems of inequality work together to produce injustice (Collins 2000), my research shows that teachers think about race and gender as very different entities. This allowed for almost all the teachers in this study to express concern about continued racial inequality in schooling while simultaneously claiming that gender inequality was no longer a major problem.

Given that Americans tend to place much faith in education as a means of addressing practically every social ill, it is imperative that we understand how teachers' attitudes about race and gender inform how they address (or avoid) race- and gender-related issues in the contemporary color- and gender-blind classroom, particularly as they pertain to the implementation of new educational policies (chapter two). As Thandeka Chapman argues (2008), "To further current conversations on successful reform implementation, research that considers the affects of large-scale policy initiatives on classroom practices is necessary. Educators, policy makers, and researchers need to understand how and why policies are embraced or rejected by teachers and students in individual schools and classrooms." (43) In order to do this effectively, I believe requires the insights of institutional ethnography. Indeed, because the methodological strategies used in this research are central to situating teachers within a complex web of interactions, a rigid hierarchy of authority, and bureaucratic policies and practices, I include a brief discussion of institutional ethnography as the model of inquiry in the next section.

THE IMPORTANCE OF INSTITUTIONAL ETHNOGRAPHY FOR STUDYING RACE AND GENDER IN SCHOOLING

Traditional sociological analysis has a long and troubling history of marginalizing, problematizing, and rendering invisible, oppressed groups. As a result, a number of alternative methodologies have been suggested to address the inherent biases in traditional approaches to studying oppression. For example, Eduardo Bonilla-Silva and Gianpaolo Baiocchi (2008) argue that research on whites' racial attitudes relies too heavily on the collection of survey data and call for greater use of in-depth interviews and mixed-method approaches. Joey Sprague (2005) contends that in order to create knowledge that is more complete and less biased toward elite views, "we need to ground each view of the social world in the standpoint from which it is created, and foster dialogue among those developing the picture from different social positions." (2)

Institutional ethnography offers a critical model of inquiry that takes up both of these challenges. The social is the focus of sociological inquiry in institutional ethnography and is reflected in people's coordinated activities with others; it is an aspect of what people do to be explored and explained (Smith 2005). According to Dorothy Smith, who first developed institutional ethnography:

> The overall aim of institutional ethnography has a double character. One is to produce for people what might be called "maps" of the ruling relations and specifically the institutional complexes in which they participate in whatever fashion.... The second aim is to build knowledge and methods of discovering the institutions and, more generally, the ruling relations of contemporary Western society. (51)

While traditional ethnography seeks to study a "site," institutional ethnography examines how that site is *held together* by other institutions (Sprague 2005). This includes institutions like gender (Lorber 1994; Risman 1998) and race (Omi and Winant 1994; Mills 1997; Bobo 1999; Bonilla-Silva 2006; Feagin 2006).

In fact, there are a number of foundational concepts that set institutional ethnography apart from traditional methods as a model for studying the social world in general, and systems of inequality and privilege in particular. The first is standpoint (Smith 2005). According to Smith, "Institutional ethnography takes for granted that each person is unique; each has a biography and experience that is her or his own; each is positioned differently from the others; each therefore sees things from a different perspective, feels things differently, has different needs and desires, different interests." (61) While institutional ethnographers acknowledge that individuals are the best authorities on their everyday practices, they do not treat experiential accounts as unblemished depictions of reality; what becomes data for the ethnographer is always a collaborative product (Smith 2005: 124; see also Campbell and Gregor 2004; Sprague 2005).

A second concept concerns institutional ethnography's analytic emphasis on organization and structure. While institutional ethnography begins by exploring the experiential accounts of the individuals connected to an institutional setting, it is not the individuals who are the objects of study (Smith 2005; Holstein 2006). The empirical goal in institutional ethnography is to elucidate social processes that have generalizing effects, not to generalize from experiential accounts (Holstein 2006). In order to achieve this goal, the ethnographer takes these accounts of everyday life as problematic, offering insights into actual circumstances where individuals participate in the social organization of those circumstances often unknowingly (Campbell and Gregor 2004: 49).

The final concept concerns the importance of texts for doing institutional ethnography. Because of the significant power of texts to organize and reveal what are essentially translocal knowledges and activities that are taken to be local and context-dependent (DeVault 2006), the analysis and critique of texts is critical to this model of inquiry (Smith 1990; Campbell and Gregor 2004; Smith 2005). Put simply, the significance of texts for institutional ethnographers is found in their ability to organize and enable social relations (Walby 2007). Texts in institutional ethnography are therefore not conceptualized as data in a traditional social science sense, nor are they limited to print media (Walby 2005). With the importance of these concepts in mind—standpoint, organization and structure, and texts—I entered the world of educators and children in order to explore teachers' attitudes and behaviors in the context of contemporary color- and gender-blind ideologies, policies, and practices.

RESEARCH DESIGN

During the 2010-2011 school year, I interviewed, observed, and then interviewed a second time, eighteen teachers who work at three different elementary schools within the same school district in a suburb north of Chicago: Morgan Elementary, Mason Elementary, and Helis Elementary, all of which offer instruction in kindergarten through fifth grade. Semi-structured initial interviews allowed me to gather background information on each teacher before observation (Appendix A). In these interviews, teachers were asked about their unique educational and career trajectory, teaching philosophy and pedagogy, as well as their subjective understanding of their social location. Several questions from the initial interview schedule were adapted from Dan Lortie's (1975) classic study of teachers and the teaching profession.

Formal observations of teachers in their classrooms included approximately fifteen hours. In almost all the classrooms, I served as a participant observer to some degree whether tying a shoelace or administering a spelling test. During these observations, I was able to record not only how teachers interacted with their students, but also other teachers, parents and administrators. This allowed me to observe how teachers addressed (and avoided) race- and gender-related issues within different contexts as well as circumstances in which the countervailing effects of privilege were particularly salient (chapter five). In this phase of the research, I also incorporated the analysis of texts that included both curricular materials, rules regarding classroom etiquette and activities, as well as physical aspects of the classrooms and the schools. In the end, formal observations comprised 253 hours of collected fieldwork data. This does not, however, include almost three hundred additional hours of informal interactions with teachers, parents, and students across all three schools. In fact, once final interviews were completed I devoted the remaining two months of the school year to working as a volunteer kindergarten aide in Mr. Williams' classroom. In sum, I spent four to five days each week in one or more of the schools throughout the academic year.

After the formal period of observation was concluded, I conducted a second semi-structured interview that asked about teacher's attitudes toward educational policy in general and race- and gender-based policies specifically (Appendix B). This final interview also allowed me to ask questions about specific events I observed while in the teachers' classrooms and for teachers' feedback regarding the data collected during this period. Teachers were compensated fifty dollars at the conclusion of the final interview to purchase classroom supplies. To protect their anonymity, all teachers' names as well the names of the schools in which they work, the school district, and the name of the community in which these schools are located have all been changed.

THE TEACHERS

After gaining permission from the principal of each school in this study to conduct my research, teachers were contacted by e-mail and telephone to ask for their participation. In the end, eight teachers volunteered to take part at Morgan, four at Mason, and six at Helis. Like the schools in which they work, the teachers in this study are diverse on several important measures. First, the teachers vary in terms of gender and age (Table 1.1). Of the eighteen teachers in this study, twelve are women and six are men. The youngest teacher is twenty-five while the oldest is sixty-one; the average teacher age is 50-years-old. Second, the teachers identify with several racial and ethnic groups including white, Black, Hispanic, Middle Eastern, Asian, and biracial (Table 1.1). Further, three white female teachers are interracially married; two to Hispanic men, a third to an African American man. All three women have biracial children.

Third, teachers also vary in terms of their social class backgrounds. Based on the level of education and the occupation of their father and mother, their family of origin household composition and other pertinent information teachers provided about their upbringing, eight teachers grew up in upper-middle class households, four in middle-class households, and six in working-class households. Because of the significant relationship between social

Table 1.1. Teachers' Gender, Race, School, Grade Level, and Curricular Program

Teacher	Gender	Race/Ethnicity	School	Grade Level	Curricular Program
Chang	Woman	Asian	Helis	3	General Education
Foy	Man	White	Morgan	4	General Education
Gira	Man	White	Morgan	5	General Education
Gold	Man	Middle Eastern	Morgan	3	General Education
Hamilton	Man	White	Morgan	3	General Education
Hurley	Woman	White	Mason	3	General Education
Jackson	Woman	White	Helis	5	General Education
Lee	Woman	Biracial	Helis	2	Inclusion
Lopez	Woman	Hispanic	Morgan	3	Dual Language
Martin	Woman	Black	Helis	2	General Education
Mendez	Woman	White	Morgan	1	Dual Language
Norman	Woman	White	Helis	5	General Education
Parker	Woman	White	Morgan	2	General Education
Roberts	Woman	White	Morgan	1	General Education
Smith	Woman	White	Mason	5	Dual Language
Stevens	Woman	White	Helis	2	Dual Language
Swain	Man	Black	Mason	3	General Education
Williams	Man	Biracial	Mason	K	General Education

class, (Lareau 1987; Carbonara 1998) race, (Cole and Omari 2003; Lareau 2003; Hardaway and McLoyd 2008) and gender (Dumais 2002; Lent and Figueira-McDonough 2002; Bettie 2003), the heterogeneity of social class background among the teachers in this study is particularly important (chapter five).

Fourth, teachers have different years of experience in the classroom. The shortest time spent teaching is 4 years, the longest is 31; the average number of years teaching is 22 years. Fifth, teachers work with different grade level children; one teaches kindergarten, two teach first grade, three teach second grade, six teach third grade, one teaches fourth grade, four teach fifth grade, and one teaches part-time in a second grade classroom and part-time in a third grade-classroom (Table 1.1). Finally, teachers work in different District 21 curricular programs; thirteen teach in the general education curriculum, four teach in the dual language program, and one is a special education/inclusion teacher (Table 1.1).

While important differences exist among the teachers, they are also similar in a number of ways that point to their access to privilege as well as their engagement in very heteronormative and homonormative (Duggan 2002) lifestyles. First, every teacher except one in this study has a master's degree; some teachers have more than one, and the one teacher who does not have a master's degree has a law degree. Second, most of the teachers are married, including one male teacher who is married to a same-gender partner. Of the only four teachers who are not currently married, one is engaged, one is divorced, and two are in long-term relationships, one of which is a cohabiting relationship with a man she refers to as her "husband."

Third, almost all of the teachers in this study have children, some who are school age, others who are grown. Of the four teachers who do not currently have children, one is in the process of trying to conceive a child with his wife; another is trying with his partner to find a birth mother; and the one teacher who is engaged plans to have children one day. There are only two teachers in this study who do not have children and do not expect to. Fourth, almost all of the teachers in this study were raised in traditional families with married fathers and mothers, siblings present, and, in the case of one teacher, grandparents as well. Only three teachers grew up in non-traditional households; two teachers grew up in a female-headed divorced household and one lived part of her childhood with her grandmothers and part with her parents.

LAKEVIEW

The schools in which the teachers in this study work are located in the District 21 public school system in Lakeview, Illinois, a suburb north of Chicago. There are two overarching reasons why I selected District 21 to conduct this research. First, as a former resident of Lakeview with children who attended District 21 schools (not included in this study), I anticipated my connection to the community and school system as well as insider knowledge of locally recognized discourses and practices, especially regarding educational policies, procedures and politics, would allow me somewhat easier entrée into the field, and tools to establish greater rapport with administrators, teachers, and students.

The second reason concerns the uniqueness of the community itself; Lakeview's population of approximately 75,000 residents is racially diverse and politically liberal; as compared with national averages, residents, for example, have a much higher level of formal education; and the town prides itself on an ethos of social justice. One might reasonably expect that a city with these demographic features would house a public school system structured for equality (e.g., Noguera 2008). Yet, like most cities Lakeview is very racially segregated and this segregation is, of course, reflected in the populations and student test scores of most of its ten public elementary schools.

SCHOOL DISTRICT 21

According to a Chicago newspaper that calculated performance indicators of Illinois public schools based on each school's 2009 state report card, one-third of District 21 schools rank among the highest performing Illinois schools. District 21 is also credited with a recent innovation that links student achievement to teacher evaluations and tenure, a tactic employed to increase the district's chances of securing a Race To The Top grant (which it was not awarded). According to the 2010 Illinois District Report Card, the average class size in the district ranges between 17.1 and 20.4 students, and per pupil expenditure is approximately $14,000, which is higher than state and national averages. Further, District 21 offers two magnet programs racial in structure if not necessarily intent: the African-Centered Curriculum (ACC) program at Mason, and a dual language program at five elementary schools including Morgan, Helis, and Mason. According to the District 21 Student Handbook (2009-2010), the ACC program "integrates historical experiences of Africans and African Americans into core curriculum and district learning standards. Low student class sizes, strong family involvement, and culturally responsive instruction to develop a deeper understanding of the African and African American cultures are features of the program." The dual language program provides instruction in both English and Spanish to enhance the academic achievement of English Language Learners (ELL). There are no gender-based curricular programs within District 21, though single-sex physical education classes begin in middle school.

THE SCHOOLS

While similarities in curricula, teacher quality, and use of best practices can be found across all three schools, Morgan, Mason, and Helis differ in important ways including racial composition (Table 1.2). Morgan is a predominantly white school; white students comprise 65% of the student body. Indeed, in order to increase racial diversity, Morgan is the only school in District 21 that includes in its attendance area a predominantly Black and Hispanic neighborhood that does not border the immediate area of the school, which is almost all white. Mason, on the other hand, is a predominantly Black school with 45% of students identifying as Black or African American. The next largest demographic group at Mason is Hispanic students who account for approximately 27% of the student body. In addition, Mason enrolls the smallest percentage of white students in District 21, approximately 20% of the student body. Finally, Helis has the largest population of Hispanic students in the district, accounting for approximately 35% of the student body; Black students comprise one-fifth and white students comprise just over one-third.

There are also stark differences between all three schools in terms of students' socioeconomic standing, the number of students who are English Language Learners (ELL), and the number of students who qualify for an Individualized Education Program (IEP) as mandated by the Individuals with Disabilities Education Act (IDEA) (Table 1.3). Students with IEPs receive special education services. At Morgan, 29% of students are considered low-income based on factors such as the number of students who qualify for free and reduced-price lunches, live in families supported by public aid, and/or live in foster care or institutions. By comparison, at Mason 65% of students are considered low-income as are 50% of students at Helis. Both of these schools are designated Title I schools. Further, while only 12% of students at Morgan are eligible for transitional bilingual programs based on limited English skills, Mason has 17% percent, and Helis has the largest proportion of limited English speakers in District 21 with 27% of the student population designated ELL. Finally, while approximately 8% of students at Morgan and

Table 1.2 Racial Composition of Morgan Elementary, Mason Elementary, and Helis Elementary

School	White	Black	Hispanic	Other
Morgan Elementary	65%	14%	12%	9%
Mason Elementary	20%	45%	27%	8%
Helis Elementary	37%	21%	34%	8%

10% percent of students at Mason have IEPS in place, at Helis 17% percent of students receive special education services.

Important differences also exist across all three schools with regard to the test scores used to determine adequate yearly progress (AYP) according to No Child Left Behind (NCLB) guidelines. Morgan Elementary, for example, is one of two District 21 schools that recently received Academic Excellence Awards for sustaining high performance over time on the Illinois Standards Achievement Test (ISAT). Specifically, test scores must demonstrate over 90% of students meet or exceed state standards to receive one of these awards. Also, because Morgan consistently receives high scores, it is ranked as one of the top public elementary schools in the state of Illinois.

Mason Elementary and Helis Elementary, on the other hand, continue to struggle in their attempts to meet AYP, though Mason did recently receive an Illinois Spotlight School Award. Spotlight awards are given to schools where over half of the student body comes from low-income families and at least 70% of students pass the ISAT in reading and mathematics. Helis, however, recently had to offer students the option to transfer to three other schools in the district including Mason because as a Title I school it failed two years in a row to make AYP. Interestingly, because Morgan Elementary currently exceeds student capacity it was not a transfer option. Helis is at a particular disadvantage when it comes to performance on the ISAT since it has the largest proportion of bilingual students in the district. While ISAT test directions may be given in Spanish, and linguistically modified language exams can be used for math and science, they cannot be used for reading. In essence, limited English speakers, unless they have attended a U.S. school for less than a year, are required to comprehend and complete the ISAT just as native English speakers.

MAPPING THE RULING RELATIONS

In 1976, Samuel Bowles and Herbert Gintis wrote, "The education system, perhaps more than any other contemporary social institution, has become the

Table 1.3 English Language Learners, Students with Individualized Education Programs, and Low Income Students at Morgan Elementary, Mason Elementary, and Helis Elementary

School	English Language Learners	Individualized Education Programs	Low Income
Morgan Elementary	12%	8%	29%
Mason Elementary	17%	10%	65%
Helis Elementary	27%	17%	50%

laboratory in which competing solutions to the problems of personal liberation and social equality are tested and the arena in which social struggles are fought out." (114) Today, education remains a popular policy solution for addressing social inequalities; indeed, it is often considered a panacea for racism and sexism. This belief is predicated on several fundamental assumptions reflective of color- and gender-blind ideologies: (1) racism and sexism are individual-level problems; (2) the education system in the U.S. is structured for equality; (3) racism and sexism are irrational; (4) education necessarily mitigates ignorance; and (5) teachers and administrators are race- and gender-neutral. Yet, empirical evidence has shown that racism and sexism are structural in nature (Lorber 1994; Bonilla-Silva 2006); grave disparities exist within the institution of education in the U.S. (Oakes 1985; Valenzuela 1999; Kozol 2005; Delpit 2006); dominant group members have a rational interest in maintaining social inequalities (Lipsitz 2006); education can actually provide more effective strategies for masking racism and sexism as opposed to challenging them (Kane and Kyrro 2001); and finally, teachers and administrators are not only influenced by cultural assumptions regarding race and gender but often perpetuate these assumptions whether deliberate or not (Foster 1990; Ferguson 2001).

In reality, education much like "race" and "gender" reflects a number of interesting paradoxes. On the one hand, education is assumed to be a great equalizer, a vehicle for social mobility. On the other hand, scholars have argued that education is in many ways a failing system that instead of "equalizing" actually perpetuates inequalities and reproduces privilege (Weber 1946; Sorokin 1956; Tyack 1974; Bowles and Gintis 1976; Bourdieu 1977; Collins 1979; Oakes 1985; Coleman and Hoffer 1987; Gutmann 1987; Valenzuela 1999; Yosso 2002; Blau 2003; Duncan 2005; Kozol 2005; Delpit 2006; Harry and Klinger 2006).

This book explores the paradoxes of education, race and gender, as I follow eighteen teachers carrying out their roles as educators in an era of color- and gender-blind politics. Because there are a number of contentious issues converging simultaneously in these teachers' everyday lives, this is a book comprised of several interrelated stories all being told at the same time. On the one hand, this is a story about teachers who care deeply about their students but are generally oblivious to the ways in which their words and behaviors reinforce dominant narratives about race and gender, constructing for their students a worldview in which race and gender do not matter despite their students' lived experiences demonstrating otherwise. This is a story about dedicated, overworked teachers who are trying to keep their heads above water while meeting the myriad demands placed upon them in a climate of high-stakes testing. This is a story about the disconnect between those who mandate educational policy like superintendents and school boards and the teachers who are expected to implement those policies often with little or no input and few resources. This is ultimately a story, however, about how the institution of education itself operates in a "post-racial" and "post-gendered" society.

Employing the insights of institutional ethnography, in the following chapters I attempt to map the ruling relations and organizational complexes in which teachers participate every day with the hope that it can get us one step closer to answering the fundamental question: how do those of us concerned about social inequalities address issues of race and gender in schooling in an era of post-racial and post-gendered politics? Constructing this map begins with exploring teachers' attitudes towards race and gender, particularly how they use the frames of color-blind racism and gender-blind sexism to explain both. Because I found teachers' perspectives on race and gender to be fundamentally different, I address each in separate chapters. Specifically, in chapter two, I examine how color-blind ideologies lead to racialized outcomes when teachers try to implement informal and formal policies that are *supposed* to be race-neutral on the surface. I also explore teachers' perspectives on the role of multiculturalism in the contemporary color-blind classroom. Chapter three illuminates how teachers' attitudes towards gender differ from their attitudes towards race, and the consequences of these differences in the gender-blind classroom. In particular, I examine how teachers use gender-blind sexism to brand gender inequality in schooling a non-problem and denigrate feminism. I also raise questions as to the effects color- and gender-blind ideologies may have on the construction of a "sexuality-blind" classroom.

In chapters four and five the map of ruling relations crystallizes as I provide a context for understanding the attitudes and behaviors of teachers revealed in chapters two and three. Both chapters locate teachers within a system of ruling relations in which they are simultaneously at the mercy of the institution and agents of the institution. As such, chapter four focuses on how three recent policy decisions mandated by the superintendent and school board compromise teachers' autonomy, authority, and power in the classroom. Chapter five reveals the countervailing effects of three types of privilege that undermine teachers' potential to serve as social justice advocates in the classroom: privilege associated with their roles as institutional experts, the privilege of white students and their families in the district, and the privilege associated with the community itself.

Finally, in chapter six, I discuss the obstacles to equality that exist in the current education system and raise the question as to whether teachers should be let off the hook for addressing race and gender inequality in schooling. I also offer a critique of No Child Left Behind as well as some considerations for future policy reform. In particular, I highlight the importance of listening to teachers when developing new educational initiatives since they are the ones on the frontlines everyday.

As Debra Hooks and Maja Miskovic (2011) point out, "In the current climate of accountability and proclamations that all children can and should learn, we are witnessing a disparity between equality talk and inequity reality." (191) I argue this disconnect will likely remain as long as current educational policies remain rooted in color- and gender-blind ideologies. Indeed, I believe the first step in addressing current racial and gender inequality in schooling is to take account of how these ideologies actually undermine teachers' potential to serve as social justice advocates in the classroom. In the following chapters, I build a case for decentering these ideologies as I problematize the social equality maxim and question the efficacy of color- and gender-blind classrooms.

Chapter Two

Race in the Color-Blind Classroom: Multiculturalism and Tracking

We need to stop thinking about this, even though it exists. We have to pretend that it doesn't exist. This, this "race thing." And just move beyond that. [Students must say to themselves] I have a goal and no matter what, I want to achieve it. And education is *it*. And I have to push myself real hard to get what I want, you know, coming to school. I, I focus, do what I need to do, and just-doesn't matter what's going on around me.

Ms. Martin, Second Grade General Education Teacher, Helis Elementary

Ms. Martin's words, spoken passionately during a conversation she and I had one afternoon in her classroom while her students were at lunch, offers a number of important insights into how teachers think about race and racial inequality in the current era of post-racial and post-gendered politics. It also illustrates how teachers construct the contemporary color-blind classroom. First, Ms. Martin lays the foundation; she acknowledges that a "race thing" does exist, but it is what she says we need to do about it that is paramount: *pretend* that it does not. Brick by brick she begins to build the walls upon that foundation by (1) reifying education as the means to achieve social equality; (2) reinforcing the notion that society is a meritocracy—if students work hard, focus, do what they need to do—they will overcome any obstacles in their paths; and (3) dismissing the impact of social location on students' potential for success. What is also insightful about this conversation is that these are the words spoken by the only Black classroom teacher at Helis Elementary, a teacher who shared with me firsthand experiences of racial inequality; a teacher who expressed to me her concerns about seeing Black boys sitting in front of the office on a regular basis, but rarely white boys; a teacher who told me stories about how other teachers and administrators would send Black children to her classroom "to handle" because she "just had a way with them." Yet, in Ms. Martin's opinion, the best way to deal with these issues is to adopt a color-blind mentality, to act like race no longer matters, to "pretend it does not exist" (e.g., Bonilla-Silva 2006).

Ms. Martin's logic reflects the paradoxical nature of race in the U.S: it is pervasive yet "invisible," invisible yet "obvious." The institutions in which the teachers in this study work, the ethos of the Lakeview community itself, and the teachers' personal beliefs and experiences, converge in myriad ways to reflect and reproduce these paradoxes. On the one hand, in District 21 "race" does not exist; after all, the social equality maxim is predicated on the belief that every student can learn and be successful regardless of social location. On the other hand, teachers are forced to acknowledge race because No Child Left Behind (NCLB) requires educators to address inequalities among students or face mandated penalties, and disparities in test scores in District 21 clearly manifest along racial lines. Further, because Lakeview prides itself on being a racially progressive community, teachers are encouraged and expected to celebrate racial diversity. The end result is that anything negative associated with race such as acknowledging the existence of institutional discrimination and white privilege that call into question the basic tenets of the social equality maxim are off-limits; anything positive associated with race such as the recognition of Hispanic Heritage month is embraced and heralded as examples of the social progressiveness of District 21 and the Lakeview community. The contradictions teachers face in having to deny the problems of race while at the same time confront them are numerous.

For example, to minimize the consequences of racism requires whites to minimize the consequences of privilege. I witnessed this occur in almost every initial interview with white teachers. When white teachers were asked to identify their race, it was as if no one wanted to admit they were white (see also Solomon et al. 2005; Marx and Larson 2012). Only one white teacher, in fact, identified herself as simply being "white." Others like Ms. Hurley referred to herself as a "citizen of the world" and "just one of the many colors in my classroom." Mr. Hamilton told me that when he was asked for his race he identified himself as a human being. In contrast to white teachers, racial minority teachers did not hesitate in identifying themselves as African-American, Black, Hispanic, Asian or biracial.

Interestingly, a dialectical relationship exists between white teachers' reluctance to acknowledge their own identity in the racial order and the various racial groups represented by their students. Sometimes teachers found creative ways to speak of the racial diversity in their classrooms without acknowledging race; Mr. Hamilton was fond of referring to his students as a million different flavors. Ms. Hurley, on the other hand, claimed to not see race at all:

Ms. Hurley: You know, people say to me, how many Black children do you have? I don't think of them that way. I have to look at the pictures.

LCS: Do people ask that because they know you teach at Mason?

Ms. Hurley: Sometimes. Sometimes. But I don't know how many. I have to like look at pictures of their names and think.

As Ms. Hurley and I exchanged this dialogue, I could not help but think of Lisa Delpit's (2006) words: "…if one does not see color, then ones does not really see children." (177) Indeed, what are the consequences of teaching children they can be anything they want to be regardless of social location when the children's lived experiences so often demonstrated otherwise?

Further, the "do's" and "don'ts" of color-blind racial etiquette created numerous incongruities for the white teachers, creating a *now-you-see-race-now-you-don't* environment. In an example below, Ms. Hurley, who denied seeing the race of her students, talks about the benefits of racial diversity within her third grade teaching team due in part to their racial differences:

We're very interesting because, you know, we've got a Black male, Black female, Columbian female, and a Caucasian, Eastern European female so it's like, it's like, we're like an interesting team. We're all demographically different!

Regardless of their race, every teacher I worked with attempted to create a color-blind classroom for their students in order to realize the social equality maxim. The color-blind classroom was intended to serve as a microcosm of the larger society, an environment where opportunities were equitable regardless of students' social locations, every child was equally loved and valued, put simply the "problems" of race were illusory. Indeed, in order to legitimate the color-blind classroom institutional discrimination could not exist. Therefore, when contradictions threatened the myth of racial equality, the teachers were compelled to acknowledge and address infractions at the individual-level. This includes teachers like Ms. Parker, who not only voluntarily took part in an anti-bias curriculum training series, but had firsthand experience of racial prejudice as someone married interracially and the mother of a biracial child. When a racial epithet was hurled at a Black girl in Ms. Parker's second grade class at Morgan, she responded not by problematizing white privilege and ongoing racial inequality, but by incorporating several books that celebrated African American hair into her literacy curriculum.

LCS: How has the reading unit on hair gone?

Ms. Parker: It's been really great! It's been really interesting. There was another incident after that one [the initial incident] about one of the kids from-
and unfortunately both of these things happened from kids outside of our
room—so at recess they're putting these things on a couple of my students.
But they said to one of my girls, you know, "you're dirty. That's why your
skin is brown." I'm like, really?!? Really?!? So.... (sighs) Um, you know, we
talked about it as a class, talked about it with that teacher, and offered her all
my skin color books and, you know, it's all you can do.

Ms. Parker's approach to addressing racial prejudice against one of her students is indeed "all you can do" in a color-blind classroom. If institutional
racism does not exist, if society is believed to be post-racial, then clearly
there is no space, incentive, or support for teachers to challenge these types
of inequality. This compels teachers to address instances of racism when they
occur at the individual-level while larger systems of privilege and oppression
go unexamined and therefore unattended (see also Sleeter 2012).

There are other consequences that result from the construction of color-
blind classrooms as well. Particularly troubling, I believe, is the adoption of a
brand of multiculturalism that further obscures the reality of contemporary
racism and perpetuates white privilege, and the development of what I refer
to as the *new face of tracking* in schools: homogenous tracking within as
opposed to across classrooms. I take up both of these issues in this chapter.
However, first I explore teachers' attitudes about race and racial inequality in
order to provide a context for understanding how multiculturalism and tracking get implemented in District 21.

TEACHERS' PERSPECTIVES ON RACE AND RACIAL
INEQUALITY IN SCHOOLING

As the manifestation of the social equality maxim, the color-blind classroom
reflects and reinforces teachers' understandings of the relationship between
race and schooling. The teachers in this study knew racial inequality existed;
with the exception of one, all the teachers I worked with regardless of their
race and the racial population of their schools, agreed with the notion that
racial inequality was still a significant problem in schooling. In fact, a few
teachers, like Mr. Hamilton, a third grade general education teacher at Morgan, told me in no uncertain terms that enduring racial inequality was the
most significant problem in education today:

It should be the most major civil rights issue right now, is, is racial inequalities
in education. Um, the reality that, that if you take a look at who is not achieving well in my classroom and you take a look at what race they are, it's
inexcusable. It is absolutely inexcusable. I would say that here at Morgan, and
one of the unique, the weird thing is we have a district where our Morgan

boundaries are not contiguous. We have this little square of land in a poorer area of Lakeview that kids are bused from every single day. And I do not have an answer to this question, but sometimes I think the best thing that could have happened for some of our students is that they happened to live in that little postage stamp of land that gets to come over here to one of the best schools in the state as measured by data. We know that. And, and so I think Anton [African American student in Mr. Hamilton's class] sure did get lucky that, that he has the right address to get here at Morgan. Um, and…so do I think there's racial inequalities, and do they remain? Absolutely and it still is affecting what we do in schools! I think we've taken a lot of efforts here in Lakeview to address that very honestly, um, but it's still nagging and it's still…not solved by any means.

While Mr. Hamilton spoke passionately about enduring racial inequality in schooling, he failed to connect his concerns to the broader context of institutional discrimination. For example, his gratitude that his students of color are bused to Morgan even though they live in a non-contiguous neighborhood which is almost all Black and Hispanic, does not question the patterns of residential segregation that explain why these students of color have to be bused to an almost all-white neighborhood school in order to obtain a modicum of racial parity at Morgan. Indeed, Mr. Hamilton situates the poor families who live in that non-contiguous neighborhood as the "lucky ones."

In the end, the tenuousness of the color-blind classroom forces teachers to walk a tightrope between openly acknowledging ongoing racial inequality and maintaining the illusion for their students that the historical problems of race have been solved and what problems remain can be accounted for by ignorance on the part of racist *individuals* and overcome by students making "good" choices. In fact, a core belief in the color-blind classroom is that students can be anything they want to be if they make good choices. The language of *good choices*, a reflection of abstract liberalism (Bonilla-Silva 2006), was used to some degree in every class I observed in relation to choosing a partner, following the rules of the classroom, and in being successful in life.

Teachers not only used the logic of abstract liberalism to buttress their understandings of race and racial inequality. A number of teachers also relied heavily on the minimization of racism frame to explain the nature and extent of contemporary racial discrimination in schooling (Bonilla-Silva 2006). The tables had turned and social class was now a greater determinate of life chances than race (e.g., Wilson 1978). Indeed, Mr. Gold, a fourth grade teacher at Morgan, told me that class now completely trumped race in terms of academic outcomes:

I think economic, economic background is [more important than race in explaining inequality] because I have kids of different races, I have African American kids that come from very successful homes, economically successful homes, and I have kids that don't. And there's also academic differences between them. So it's not even the race, it's just economics. Where kids come from, you know. So…it's present but we work very hard to even it out, even the field.

Unlike Mr. Gold, however, most teachers who emphasized the importance of class acknowledged that race was still a problem, but it was declining in significance when compared to socioeconomic status (e.g.,Wilson 1978):

LCS: Do you think racial inequality is still a problem in schooling?

Mr. Foy: Well, again, it depends on what you mean. Unequal treatment, unequal opportunity, unequal attitudes by teachers toward students? Um, I think if they still exist they're much more subtle than they used to be. In some sense, I guess, that's progress. That it's kind of been driven underneath, and maybe it's diminished over the years. I think it's fair to say, um, I think that inequalities nowadays are more economic. So African American kids who are struggling academically are in general coming from the lower income homes, um, not as educated, undereducated homes. Kids who are coming from affluent educated households, um, I think—this is just my own personal—are, are succeeding as much as, uh, white kids are.

LCS: So you would say a problem exists, but it appears to be class-based, or socioeconomic?

Mr. Foy: I think. Now, that's here in Lakeview, and I suspect many places. I am sure many other places the problem is, um, unequal, unequal attitudes, attitudes towards kids that are not fair and, and sometimes they're hard to-people will deny they have those attitudes, but if you dig a little bit deeper, you could kind of see it, um, or it becomes obvious that, yes, there is a racial attitude or, or a, a belief that those kids aren't going to achieve, so therefore I'm not going to put much energy into having them achieve.

Mr. Foy stumbles over a number of contradictions in this exchange as he attempts to maintain his balance on the tightrope. First, he questions whether racial inequality still exists; then acknowledges a basic tenet of color-blind racism: the evolution of racial discrimination from overt to more covert forms; then uses the minimization of racism frame to explain current racial disparities; and then finally acknowledges that covert forms of discrimination probably do still exist, but not in Lakeview. Instead, social class is offered as the primary explanation for inequality: students who come from lower socioeconomic backgrounds regardless of race are disadvantaged and students who come from higher socioeconomic backgrounds regardless of race are advantaged. Yet, this logic ignores the fact that students coming from lower socioeconomic backgrounds in District 21 are overwhelming racial and ethnic minorities. Here, poverty is essentially treated as race-neutral. Further, this logic overestimates the effects of social class in mitigating the consequences of race: "While blacks have come closer to parity with whites in income, education, and occupation, the substantial racial differences in wealth continue to affect educational and social opportunities." (Orr 2003: 299) According to Amy Orr, the disparities in wealth between white and Black households explain in large part the enduring discrepancies in standardized tests scores between white and Black students.

While the negative effects of poverty on student opportunities and outcomes were a common concern expressed by most of the teachers I worked with, sometimes teachers also discussed culture (Bonilla-Silva 2006) as an important variable that distinguished the students in their class. In the following Ms. Hurley acknowledges the importance of race and class in understanding inequality, but adds that culture is also a critical factor:

> I do think it's an issue [race]. I think perceptions, any time you have, um...any time you have, um, minority students especially low-income minority students, you know. You're talking about challenges there that might be different because of, partly because of class, and it doesn't matter whether you're Black or white, but also because of culture. Um, and you know those differences, um, can impact how children learn, what their style is, you know. Um, it, it took me a while to get used to, uh, low loud African American females are. White girls tend to be quiet, I mean, this is as stereotype, of course, you know. I don't generally say, "Oh, it's a white child, she's going to be quiet or blonde, she's going to be stupid." No, no, no, no. But I've just noticed, you know, that, that the high, well, it's kind of like Italians are very high-profile. You know, I think by culture some people are. They're louder, and they express their emotions differently, you know. But, put them together and you see kind of calming of that, and I mean, let's face it. There's a social way to act on the streets and at home and with your family and there's an educational way to act just like when you have a job someday. There's a way that you act and speak and talk and dress at your job and at home you might be different. You might swear, you might wear jeans, you know, you might yell to your friends. And, and I think kids just have to learn that to be successful, so, so whether they're high-profile or not, you know, I think there's a place to meet in the middle, and for those kids that don't express themselves whether they're white or they're Latino or they're withdrawn and they're African American and whatever, you know, I think that there's a meeting in the middle that happens when you form community in a classroom. And kids start rubbing off on each other.

Ms. Hurley's dialogue offers a number of powerful insights about race in the color-blind classroom. As soon as she makes the comment about African American girls being too loud, she immediately attempts to walk it back and instead assert a much more race-neutral position to justify her argument about the importance of culture. In fact, she decides to juxtapose "how loud African American girls are" with the "high-profile" culture of Italians, substituting a racially charged example with a much more dispassionate one as she tries to disentangle race from her comments about culture. Her appearance of *neutrality* is compromised, however, when she emphasizes the *calming down* of minority children, especially Black girls, as a benefit of their interactions with white children. Also, Ms. Hurley stresses, as did many other teachers, the importance of understanding, internalizing, and obeying the rules of the "school culture" in order to be successful (as opposed to "other culture"), an important theme discussed in detail in chapter five.

Teachers also appropriated color-blind language when discussing multiculturalism as a strategy for advancing racial equality. Like with teachers' understandings of race, their understandings of multiculturalism reflected a number of interesting paradoxes. On the one hand, every teacher with whom I worked stated that any attempts to incorporate multicultural curricula into the learning environment, was supported wholeheartedly by their principals and the parents of their students. Indeed, the plausibility of the color-blind classroom was enhanced not only through the denial of institutional discrimination, but through embracing racial diversity: differences *obviously* exist among students, but differences are *always* a good thing. This was the essence of multiculturalism in District 21; and as I quickly learned, educational strategies that deviated from this brand of multiculturalism were not welcome.

THE KOREAN FAN DANCE: EMBRACING MULTICULTURALISM

Contemporary race scholars challenge that all too often current expressions of multiculturalism leave structural power dynamics such as the effects of capitalism unexamined (Darder and Torres 1998) and focus instead on increasing self-esteem among nonwhite students or improving white students' understanding of history (Bush 2004). In this way, multiculturalism often acts as another form of white privilege. In fact, according to Amanda Lewis (2005), "Multiculturalism as currently manifested not only does little to challenge students' understanding of culture, difference, and race, but in fact serves to defend the status quo." (35; see also Perry 2001)

District 21 takes great pride in considering itself a multicultural school system. In the following exchange, Mr. Hamilton expresses the overwhelming sentiment shared by the teachers I worked with regarding multiculturalism in District 21:

> LCS: Do you feel supported in your efforts to incorporate multicultural curricula in your classroom?

> Mr. Hamilton: Oh, absolutely! I think, uh, the one thing I love about teaching in Lakeview is that we are self-consciously oriented towards equity and justice-multiculturalism. I mean, the more obscure the culture the better it seems

sometimes! You know, I, if I were teaching children how to do a Korean fan dance, I'll bet you I would have very little resistance from, uh, from administration or faculty on how to do it. They would want to know what standards I was teaching, how to do it, curriculum, they would want to know those things. But they would have no objection to me doing that, um, so yeah, certainly there's a huge support for those kinds of things.

At the same time that Mr. Hamilton acknowledges the overwhelming support that teachers receive for bringing multicultural curricula into the classroom, his juxtaposition of the "obscurity" of other cultures with what he implies is the "normal" (white) culture points once again to teachers' obliviousness of privilege, if not inequality. Also note that support for multiculturalism, according to Mr. Hamilton, is contingent upon teachers justifying its legitimacy to their principals and to parents.

After spending several months talking with and observing teachers and students, attending field trips and assemblies, even just walking the school halls, it was clear to me that multiculturalism in District 21 was expressed in essentially four ways: (1) the celebration of racial and ethnic holidays and special accomplishments by people of color; (2) the placement of pictures of notable people of color on school walls as well as posters with catchy slogans extolling the virtues of diversity like "The Hand of Friendship has No Color"; (3) the incorporation of literature about people of color and/or written by people of color; and (4) enrichment opportunities including field trips and school assemblies—what Jonathan Kozol (2005) might call "token days." Multiculturalism in District 21 did not include any systematic critique of unearned privilege, white supremacy, or contemporary institutional racism. Indeed, if there was any discussion of racial injustice with students it was generally introduced through the lens of history in the context of a social studies lesson.

Further, because there was no required, explicitly defined multicultural curricular program in place within District 21, principals and teachers generally had the autonomy to determine how much of any of the four elements of multiculturalism they wanted to integrate into their schools and classrooms. In the following two general education teachers and one dual language teacher discuss the nature of multiculturalism incorporated in their classes. The examples of multiculturalism they provide are typical of the classrooms I observed.

Mr. Foy: We see it [multicultural curriculum] mostly in social studies when we study a particular topic. I think it's [the social studies curriculum] pretty good about including African and, um, Hispanic, um, elements of the culture, Native American elements. We're going to start a unit on Illinois history pretty soon and, um, and there's a focus on, um, both the experiences of Native Americans' history and the experience of African American history and Illinois history. Some of the books we read, uh, many of the books that we read, that are part of the curriculum are by African American authors about the African American experience. Um, I just finished reading aloud to my class, um, *The Watsons Go to Birmingham 1963*. We talk a lot about that. We talk a lot about the Civil Rights Movement. So it's there. Does it need to be more? I suppose. I'm sure I could do more. But I'm fairly confident that I include as much as I should.

While multiculturalism in Mr. Foy's fourth grade class occurred primarily in the context of social studies lessons, once again reinforcing the notion that racial inequality was an unfortunate consequence of history rectified by the Civil Rights Movement, multiculturalism in Mr. Hamilton's third grade class was expressed through the selection of certain texts. In the following Mr. Hamilton responds to a question I posed as to how he incorporates multiculturalism in his classroom:

Um, I, I would say being very, just cognizant of the characters that, that I'm choosing to read, you know, very cognizant of who the characters in my story are and, I'll do that where, okay, this particular, um, theme of this story happens in Mexico. The theme of this story, um, is the African American family. Um, and so I am very conscious about choosing those things.

Although Mr. Hamilton's strategy for incorporating multiculturalism in his classroom may be pedagogically different from Mr. Foy, the end result is the same. Just as Mr. Foy fails to acknowledge contemporary racism by situating institutional discrimination as historically contingent, Mr. Hamilton's attempts to celebrate racial diversity through his selection of literature while perhaps noble, glosses over enduring racial inequalities. Mr. Hamilton's words and pedagogy express the notion that race does not matter, yet in reality there remain material consequences attached to race in the U.S.

Like Mr. Hamilton, Ms. Stevens chose to emphasize what she saw as the *positive value* of racial diversity. In Ms. Stevens' classroom, for example, multiculturalism took the form of celebrating Hispanic holidays, or similar to Mr. Foy, she just "worked in" race where she thought necessary:

I mean, I've never read the official description they give to parents about dual language but I'm pretty sure it includes something about like, you know, history of Hispanic culture and things like that, and unfortunately it's not part of our current curriculum for social studies and stuff. I just try to work it in wherever I can like if there's a Hispanic holiday or like something happening in Guatemala or whatever, I try....

In the end, while all teachers expressed the importance of multiculturalism and felt there was ample support by the district and their school communities to incorporate multicultural curricula in their classrooms, there were limits even within the narrow scope of "acceptable" multiculturalism. It was perfectly defensible to read books by authors of color, celebrate Black History month, to teach students how to do a Korean fan dance. It was not permissible, however, to have an entire African-centered curriculum, at least not according to the majority of teachers in this study.

WHERE IS THE PROGRAM FOR POLISH STUDENTS? THE LIMITS OF MULTICULTURALISM

African-Centered Curriculum (ACC) is a magnet program offered at only one school in District 21, Mason Elementary, where the population of Black students is approximately forty-five percent of the total population. The ACC program was instituted in 2006 amidst controversy within the school system and the community at large. The main objection to instituting ACC was that it would reinstate formal segregation within a school district that had a long history of supporting integration; although the program would be open to applications from all District 21 students, the assumption (and later reality) was that it would be primarily if not entirely African American students who would enroll. The main endorsement for instituting ACC was that a program built on smaller class sizes, strong family involvement, and increasing the self-esteem and confidence of racial minority children through an emphasis on "culturally-relevant" curricula would decrease the disparities in test scores between white and Black students that had long plagued the district.

Very few teachers in this study, including general education teachers at Mason, knew anything substantive about ACC including its philosophical, pedagogical, and curricular foundation; everyone, however, had an opinion about the program. My intention was to build rapport with the teachers before specifically asking for their perspectives on the program, but in the case of Ms. Stevens it came up in our first meeting as we discussed the potential emphasis on Hispanic culture in the dual language program, which she strongly supported (in theory if not practice). ACC was another story:

> Well, I don't know. I just, I don't know anyone [associated with ACC], and I honestly don't know that much about it. I just think…it's like they don't have like a program for, you know, for like all the kids who are Polish, to learn together about Poland. They're not learning Polish, they're just learning about Poland. It's like why do we need a whole program just to learn about Africa? When like, I don't know. I just, I get that it's a big cultural group, but I just think if you're going to offer one for African-Americans, you should also offer one for kids who are Polish or Czechoslovakian or whatever, I don't know. That's just my opinion.

According to the 2000 Census, persons of Polish ancestry accounted for less than six percent of the population of Lakeview while African Americans made up one-fourth. I did not, however, intuit Ms. Stevens' argument as one that could be assuaged by demographic data.

Indeed, Ms. Steven's comments reflected what most teachers expressed as their overarching concern with ACC: the self-segregation of Black students within a curricular program focused on Africa and African-Americans. After all, if the social equality maxim dictated that all students were equal (interpreted by teachers as "the same"), and adopting the logic of abstract liberalism (Bonilla-Silva 2006) meant that no group should be singled out for special treatment, then why should District 21 offer the option of enrolling in a race-specific curricular program? As Mr. Gold told me:

> I'm not big on any group being singled out for anything, you know, I kind of like to be—I'm Jewish, so I don't want to be singled out as Jewish. I don't want to be singled out as anything else. Just go to the place, learn. Be American. We are Americans, you know. And that's my view of things.

Further, if District 21 was going to provide such a program, why was it geared towards *those* (Black) students as opposed to students of Polish ancestry (white students), for example? As Ms. Jackson, a fifth grade teacher at Helis, asked me, with no critical reflection of the dominance of Eurocentric curricula in the district, "Can you imagine them [District 21] saying 'we need to have a special program for white kids because they're not getting enough [attention]?'"

In the end, almost every teacher who I asked about ACC was strongly opposed on the grounds that it was essentially a segregated program. In the following, a white general education teacher at Morgan and a biracial dual language teacher at Helis share their perspectives of ACC:

> Mr. Foy: I'm not, I'm not very supportive of it. I think it promotes, um, I think it promotes segregation. I think it promotes different, you know, kids are different. I'm not exactly sure what Afrocentric education means. What are you—how are those kids that much different? How is the education that much different? Um, I think it's important to promote in our curriculum, um, models of African American achievement, and, um, teach African American history and to, um, celebrate cultural achievements of Africans and African Americans, um, maybe, maybe even slightly more so than European. But, in general, we need to celebrate in the limited time we have, celebrate the cultures and achievements of everybody.

In this excerpt, Mr. Foy goes so far as to suggest that maybe it is okay to focus on the cultural achievements of African Americans even more so than whites, but in the next breath dismisses this claim by arguing that teachers do not have much time to devote to celebrating various cultures anyway, and when they do, every racial group should get "their fair share." Once again an appeal is made to the logic of abstract liberalism (Bonilla-Silva 2006) that assumes there are no significant differences among racial groups (for example, Mr. Foy's question as to whether Black students in ACC are that *different* from their non-ACC counterparts and his dismissive tone that asserts they are not), and therefore no group should be singled out for *special treatment*, all while ignoring the pervasiveness of white privilege.

Interestingly, when I asked Ms. Lee for her perspective, she attempted to juxtapose ACC with dual language, a magnet program that she was instrumental in bringing to Lakeview:

> Well, I, I don't see it [ACC] as an inclusive model. Um, I see it as an exclusive model, and I don't personally, I don't believe in that. The dual language model which I was, I was one of the hugest, uh, biggest, most prominent, you know, pioneers, you know, for that. We gave a lot of presentations and I was the chair of many committees to get dual language into Lakeview, um, and that is an all-inclusive model. I mean, any child can participate.

To be fair, not *any* child could participate in dual language. Students who were not English language learners could apply for the magnet program (just as they could the ACC program) and were selected by lottery with preference given to students who had siblings already in the dual language program and students whose neighborhood school offered dual language. Even so, I did not take Ms. Lee's point about the inclusive nature of the dual language program as an invitation to quibble over the eligibility guidelines, but to appeal once again to the social equality maxim. In sum, the general attitude expressed by teachers when it came to multiculturalism was that it was acceptable to *add* culturally-relevant materials to the existing (white) curriculum, particularly the literacy and social studies curriculum; it was not acceptable to offer an entire curricular program focused on a specific racial (minority) group. Ms. Mendez, a first grade teacher at Morgan, encapsulates this sentiment in the following:

> I think that's [ACC] going against what you want, what you want to teach because I mean, I'm not—I don't know 100% about the program, but I know it's, you know, centered on African curriculum and, you know, teaching all about that and, I, I just don't, I don't think it's necessary to do that. I think you probably have a class, you know, about that or have, you know, have—and we do stuff with, you know, African American history month and things like that. I mean, I don't even know if I was even from Africa, I don't know that I'd want my kid in a program where that's like the main thing since there are so many other cultures and they don't really talk about them, um, and so I think what I heard from other teachers, too, like a lot of people don't want to put their kids in it because it's so dominated by one particular culture.

Interestingly, Ms. Mendez overlooks the fact that District 21's standard general education curriculum is dominated by one particular culture: that of white Americans.

Given the overwhelming negative attitudes expressed about ACC, I thought the following dialogue between Ms. Parker and myself one morning particularly insightful.

> LCS: What do you think about ACC as a strategy for addressing racial inequalities in schooling?
>
> Ms. Parker: Um...I think that...it's hard to say because they [the district] keep it under wraps a lot.
>
> LCS: How so?
>
> Ms. Parker: We don't hear anything about it. They don't share stories of it. Um, it's not talked about ever.

This exchange, of course, begs the question as to why ACC "is kept under wraps" but perhaps a more important question is whether teachers' attitudes about ACC might change if teachers throughout the district were provided regular, substantive information about the program. Interestingly, teachers who taught in curricular programs other than ACC at Mason were more likely to identify positive aspects of the program. However, their concerns also mirrored those of teachers in other schools. In the following a Black general education teacher at Mason offers his insights regarding ACC.

> LCS: Since you mentioned an early desire to work with African American boys, I'm curious to know if you have ever worked in the ACC program here at Mason.
>
> Mr. Swain: No, I haven't.
>
> LCS: You wanted to teach gen ed?
>
> Mr. Swain: Yes, I wanted to do that because, yeah, I feel like for me and just my experience it's—I don't want the kids to feel segregated and I don't think—I just like the diversity. I guess that's the easiest way to say it. I like the diversity of the gen ed classroom. I like to, um, the kids sort of get to see different races and backgrounds and I think that, to me, is the strongest way to teach because it's more reflective of what they see in real life, you know.

In this exchange, Mr. Swain expresses his preference for teaching in the general education curriculum due to the lack of diversity in the ACC program, a concern shared by most of the teachers in this study including those who considered themselves racially progressive. Yet, in their concerns about the "segregation" of the ACC program, none of these teachers raised the fundamental question as to *why* there were no white students interested in enrolling in ACC. Inevitably the assumption was that "diversity" was achieved by integrating students of color into general education classes, as opposed to integrating white students into ACC classes.

Despite a number of attempts to solicit participation, no teacher in the African-Centered Curriculum program volunteered to participate in this research. Although I cannot be sure of their reasoning, to be honest, I know I would be skeptical of inviting a white "outsider" in to observe the program given the widespread opposition I found among the other teachers in this study. However, the lack of feedback from ACC teachers in this study is particularly unfortunate because I think it would have allowed for some important counterclaims about the significance of this program.

COLOR-BLIND POLICIES AND THE NEW FACE OF TRACKING

While multiculturalism in District 21 offers an example of how *informal* policies are implemented in an era of post-racial and post-gendered politics, there are also several *formal* policies that illustrate this as well. In fact, one of the first things I was struck by when I began the observation phase of this research was how different the structure of classrooms in District 21 was compared to when I attended elementary school over twenty years ago. Gone were the rows of desks facing towards the front of the room where the teacher sat in his or (almost always) her position of authority, presiding over their class. Instead, in all but one of the classrooms in which I observed four or five desks were grouped together in small pods, or students sat at round or rectangular tables, all facing one another. This environment fostered what teachers called *cooperative learning.* Further, most teachers attempted to cultivate a sense of camaraderie among the students who sat together and would sometimes have students take turns serving as table captains. With the exception of one, all classrooms also contained a rug or carpet area where students, particularly those in kindergarten through fourth grade, were frequently called to sit during the day for teacher instruction or read-alouds. This gathering spot was generally located near the Promethean board, a modern technological device in all District 21 classrooms that easily replaced teachers' traditional reliance on chalkboards and allowed them to instantly bring various types of media into the classroom in real time. Finally, all classrooms contained kidney-shaped or small round tables where most of the teacher-guided small group work took place.

Yet, while it initially appeared much had changed in the contemporary elementary school classroom, I soon learned many things had not changed very much at all. Indeed, the three unique learning environments found at Morgan, Mason, and Helis lend support to the argument that despite the perceived single curriculum of the elementary school, elementary schools are rigidly tracked by socioeconomic status and administrative fiat (Entwisle, Alexander and Olson 1997). What I immediately discovered when I began my classroom observations was that homogenous tracking was also occurring on a daily basis in all three schools through the implementation of recently adopted educational policies such as differentiation, Response to Intervention (RTI) and inclusion.

Differentiation is an educational philosophy developed by Carol Ann Tomlinson. According to Tomlinson (2000):

> What we call *differentiation* is…a way of thinking about teaching and learning. As such, it is based on a set of beliefs: (1) Students who are at the same age differ in their readiness to learn, their interests, their styles of learning, their experiences, and their life circumstances; (2) The differences in students are significant enough to make a major impact on what students need to learn, the pace at which they need to learn it, and the support they need from teachers and others to learn it well; (3) Students will learn best when supportive adults push them slightly beyond where they can work without assistance; (4) Students will learn best when they can make a connection between the curriculum and their interests and life experiences; (5) Students will learn best when learning opportunities are natural; (6) Students are more effective learners when classrooms and schools create a sense of community in which students feel significant and respected; (7) The central job of schools is to maximize the capacity of each student. (7)

The basis for this set of beliefs rests heavily on Tomlinson's personal experiences as a public school teacher in the nineteen-seventies and nineteen-eighties. Further, Tomlinson places significant emphasis on brain research to buttress her claims regarding children's needs and abilities (Tomlinson and Kalbfleisch 1998).

Ironically, Tomlinson's concerns over race, class and gender inequalities in schooling served as a major impetus for the development of differentiation. In theory, differentiated learning addresses all types of disparities by challenging teachers to attend to each of their student's unique educational needs and learning styles; a basic tenet of differentiation is that a one-size-fits-all approach in the classroom does a disservice to all students particularly those who struggle and those who are gifted. Tomlinson calls on teachers to "differentiate up," providing every student with the skills and opportunities to achieve at a higher (above-average) level. Perhaps as no surprise in an era of high-stakes testing, District 21 embraced differentiation, inviting Tomlinson in the fall of 2010, to conduct a professional development seminar for its teachers and sponsoring a community speaking engagement with Tomlinson, which I attended. After Tomlinson's visit, the superintendent sent a letter to all parents of District 21 students indicating that her visit served as further validation that the district's adoption of differentiated learning as part of their five-year strategic plan was beneficial for all students and represented the future of curricular development and implementation in District 21.

There was not one teacher I worked with who disagreed with the basic premises of differentiated learning. The implementation of differentiation, however, was something most teachers found to be challenging if not impossible. After all, how does one teacher create and deliver a uniquely structured learning experience for every student in his or her class? In the end, while every teacher I observed found some success in implementing activities with their students through differentiated instruction, the challenge issued by the superintendent and school board was to create a classroom in which differentiation was occurring throughout the day, every day.

In addition to the demands placed upon them to differentiate their classrooms, teachers were also required to spend a mandated number of minutes every day working one-on-one or in small groups with RTI students. RTI is a widely adopted intervention program currently used in schools to attempt to target through ongoing formal assessments students who are at-risk due to their language arts or math skills, behavioral problems, or other areas of concern including speech or language abilities. RTI is a three-tier intervention system. Tier I consists of assessing all students to determine if they are at-risk. Students that are identified as at-risk, or in need of Tier II services, are put on an intervention program that, unlike differentiation, specifically calls for small-group work with other Tier II students. Tier III students receive more intense intervention services that can include small group or one-on-one services.

Finally, another recent policy initiative in District 21, inclusion, requires teachers to adapt learning strategies in order to fully include students who have documented behavioral, cognitive, and developmental disabilities, those students with Individualized Education Programs (IEPs), in the general education classroom. Inclusion was first introduced in District 21 in 2008 and is being rolled out by grade level. Currently, inclusion is fully implemented in kindergarten through first grade; every grade level in the district, however, includes or has the possibility of including students in general education classes with IEPs.

While support for inclusion as an alternative to traditional self-contained special education classrooms continues to grow (Idol 2006), studies have nonetheless documented concerns among teachers especially with regard to the lack of special education training on the part of general education teachers who are expected to accommodate IEP students (Burke and Sutherland 2004) and negative attitudes expressed by non-IEP students in inclusion classes (Siperstein, Parker, Bardon, and Widaman 2007). Other concerns include the consequences of incorporating students with severe behavioral problems in general education classrooms (Idol 2006), the ability of the general education teacher or special education teacher to ensure that IEP students are not marginalized among their non-IEP peers (Berry 2006), the lack of formal training among inclusion paraprofessionals who often spend a lot of one-on-one instruction time with IEP students (Suter and Giangreco 2009), and as I saw firsthand, the lack of human and financial resources to implement inclusion as is intended with two highly-qualified co-teachers who are equally responsible for instruction of the class, one a general education teacher and the other a special education teacher. Further, to carry out inclusion as intended requires co-teachers to have adequate time to effectively plan, the lack of which was something co-teachers in this study complained was a chronic problem, and the willingness of general education teachers to share control of their class, not relegate their special education co-teacher to the role of instructional aid (Volonino and Zigmond 2007). I witnessed both in my classroom observations.

In sum, for teachers and co-teachers to try to meet all the challenges of differentiation, RTI, and inclusion, they must rely heavily on grouping students together during the school day, despite the fact that these policies are in *theory* designed to attend to every child's "unique" educational needs. For example, a differentiated task is one where the goal and outcome of the activity are the same for the entire class, but understanding that students learn in different ways and at different speeds, the teacher provides a number of options for students in order to achieve the objective. A teacher who has eighteen students is not expected to develop eighteen different options to complete an assignment, as the logic of differentiation might imply. Instead, a teacher may develop three different strategies and allow his or her students to choose which path they want to take to achieve the end goal. Thus, grouping becomes a natural extension of differentiation.

Differentiation, RTI, and inclusion are not only designed *theoretically* to attend to each student's individual needs; these policies are also designed theoretically to be *race-neutral*. Yet, the implementation of these policies I found was anything but "neutral." According to Tomlinson, "Regardless of intent, acceptance of either special classes or tracks as a pervasive mechanism for addressing learner needs yields racial patterns that have become predictable in our schools." (2004: 518) Ironically, the manifestation of differentiation that I observed almost always took on these same dynamics of "traditional" tracking. The new face of tracking, however, occurs *within* as opposed to *across* classrooms. Indeed, the groupings of students I observed also took on the predictable fashion of which Tomlinson warned.

For example, while teachers were "encouraged" to group students heterogeneously (e.g., Abu El-Haj and Rubin 2009), whether working with one partner or in a small group, students were generally placed with other students that were of the same gender or race. Although teachers were very deliberate in assigning students to "pods" or tables so the grouping of students in the classroom was heterogeneous overall in terms of race and gender, when students worked on academic tasks with partners, self-selected or teacher-assigned, or with small groups other than their tablemates, they generally found themselves working with students of the same gender and race. As Jeannie Oakes pointed out in 1985, not only has research failed to show any group of students who benefits consistently from homogenous groupings, but the groupings of students that result from tracking and the consequent ways that educators tend to view these students ("good" students are found in high-achieving tracks, "bad" students are found in low-achieving tracks) produces very different experiences of schooling for students (see also Ansalone and Biafora 2010; Stromquist 2012). Ironically, even though many teachers were convinced that situating these small groups within the larger classroom obscured students' awareness of the high-achieving students and the low-achieving students—indeed, Ms. Lee who wanted to be on record as many times as possible in support of inclusion told me on more than one occasion a major goal of inclusion was to foster the *invisibility* of inclusion students in the general education classrooms—my interactions with students confirmed that teachers frequently underestimated their astuteness.

Homogenous grouping in District 21 occurs for three main reasons. First, in the case of IEP students, Black and Hispanic boys are overrepresented among students who qualify for special education services. Whether resource (special education) teachers come into the classroom to provide "push-in" services, or take the students from their classroom to receive "pull-out" services, because of the concentration of racial minority boys with IEPs, when these students receive services together they typically receive them with others of the same gender and race.

Second, teachers are expected to rely heavily on formal assessments to determine whether or not students have mastered particular objectives. The outcomes of these assessments produce categories of students who are achieving above grade level, at grade level, and below, and in general it is these groups of students who end of working together on academic tasks. Relying on formal assessments in this manner to address inequalities in schooling creates an obvious tautology. First, ISAT scores reveal disparities in achievement between white students and minority students. Differentiation, for example, is then offered as a strategy to address inequalities in achievement. Teachers rely on formal assessments to determine how students should be grouped in order to deliver differentiated instruction. Therefore, not surprisingly, the classroom assessments typically produce groupings of students that mirror the distribution in the statewide tests used to determine adequate yearly progress (AYP). The belief among educators who support differentiation is that in a differentiated classroom, students who struggle, with or without IEPs, will benefit from interaction with their higher-achiev-ing peers; yet, in my observations lower-achieving students were most often grouped with other students who also struggled when it came to reading groups, for example. Interestingly, the results of formal assessments do not produce results that would dictate same-gender groups, yet in my classroom observations it was uncommon to see mixed-gender groups of students work-ing together, and I witnessed several times teachers specifically group stu-dents by gender.

Obviously, therefore, teachers did not rely solely on formal assessments or IEPs to determine which students should be partnered or assigned to a small group. Teachers' personal assessments of their students were consid-ered just as important as formal assessments in determining which students should work together. In the following exchange Ms. Lopez, a fourth grade teacher in the dual language program at Morgan, talks very candidly about how she groups her students.

> Ms. Lopez: Well, I know their strengths. I know their strengths.
>
> LCS: Is that from formal assessments or from your personal observations?
>
> Ms. Lopez: Both. It's everything. Throw it in the pot, you know, and use it as needed.

Because teachers' personal assessments factor heavily into how they group their students, understanding teachers' attitudes towards race and gender are critical to discerning how educational policies such as differentiation, RTI, and inclusion, get implemented in the color-blind classroom.

In the end, because social location does not matter in the color- and gender-blind classroom, grouping students by race and gender is not inher-ently problematic. The reality, however, despite what teachers may believe or *want* to believe, is that their students are very aware of the dynamics of race and gender in their classes. The students I observed knew who worked together in teacher-led small groups and when receiving push-in services, as well as who left the classroom to receive pull-out services. Further, as I will show in the next chapter, when it came to gender the students would most often choose partners of the same gender when given the opportunity. There-fore, the issue is not that gender and race are *invisible* in the color—and gender-blind classroom; it is that race and gender are inconsequential. This means that homogenous tracking and non-critical multicultural add-ons that do little to challenge white privilege and contemporary institutional racism can continue as expressions of the social equality maxim with little concern about the outcomes when teachers perpetuate dominant narratives of race and gender.

CONCLUSION: TRYING REALLY HARD TO GET THERE

According to Mica Pollock (2008), there are four foundational principles for doing antiracism in schooling: (1) rejecting false notions of human difference; (2) acknowledging lived experiences shaped along racial lines; (3) learning from diverse forms of knowledge and experience; and (4) challenging systems of racial inequality (xx). When I asked the teachers in this study to define antiracism, their responses mirrored Pollock's criteria with the exception of the last principle; not surprisingly in an era of post-racial and post-gendered politics, teachers' definitions of antiracism were almost always framed as something that occurred on an *individual-level*. To synthesize their responses, an antiracist teacher is someone who has no preconceived notions about race (someone who is not prejudiced), does not treat their students favorably or unfavorably on the basis of race and indeed celebrates racial diversity (someone who supports multiculturalism), and consciously attempts to create an environment for their students that is not bound by race (the essence of the color-blind classroom).

Based on the definitions the teachers provided as well as Pollock's (2008) criteria, it was not surprising that almost everyone considered himself or herself an antiracist teacher. Some like Ms. Smith embraced the label stating that being antiracist was something she worked very hard at while others like Mr. Foy accepted the label but acknowledged their antiracism efforts could be more valiant. Interestingly, Ms. Parker, the teacher at Morgan who had taken part in the anti-bias training series, was the most self-reflective and thoughtful when I asked her if she considered herself an antiracist teacher. After a long pause, her response was, "I'm trying really hard to get there." While teachers' claims to antiracism may appear disingenuous given the aforementioned examples of homogenous tracking, the desire to minimize the consequences of racism in schooling by implicating socioeconomic status and culture as the *real* problems, and the general opposition to curricular programs that target racial minorities despite continued racial inequality, in the context of the color-blind classroom their responses makes perfect sense: color-blind logic assumes if the intent is not racial, then neither are the consequences.

This is not the end of the story, however. Yes, teachers relied heavily on the frames of color-blind racism in order to explain their understandings of race and racial inequality. Yes, teachers must be held accountable at a personal level when they make comments and behave in ways that further racial injustice. However, the institutions in which the teachers work are grounded in color-blind ideologies reflective of a "post-racial" society. This sets the expectation for how both informal policies like multiculturalism and formal policies like RTI, inclusion, and differentiation are to be carried out in the district. Teachers who adopt the social equality maxim and implement these policies in alignment with this edict are supported in their efforts; teachers who might challenge the premises on which it is based know, or at least *expect,* as they told me, they will pay a price (chapter five). This is particularly problematic for those teachers who are not yet tenured. In the end, the institutional complexes in District 21 work *against* the probability of teachers serving as social justice advocates.

For example, when I began observing in classrooms, it was immediately apparent to me a major disconnect exists between those who make educational policy and seek to enforce it including superintendents and school boards, and the classroom teachers who are expected to implement it. Elementary teachers in District 21 have myriad demands placed upon them, more than I would have ever expected, to be honest, and every teacher I worked with made numerous sacrifices to try and meet those demands including coming to school early, working long hours, giving up their lunch periods, and spending their own money on resources for their students. Further, they are expected to regularly participate in professional development seminars and to embrace new initiatives the superintendent, school board, and their principals, hand down like inclusion and differentiation, often with very little if any input.

In reality, differentiation, unlike inclusion and RTI, is not new. As a number of teachers told me, trying to meet students where they are and working with them to achieve academic growth is something they did before "differentiation" existed. What Carol Ann Tomlinson did in developing a model of differentiated learning, however, was unintentionally provide justification for a new form of tracking. Indeed, I suspect an element of differentiation that particularly appeals to educators is the emphasis on students' differences. After all, teachers are expected to exert a great deal of effort to maintain the façade that all students are the same in terms of potential and opportunity, yet they know assessments reveal stark differences between categories of students and those categories are most obvious in terms of race, and in the case of students with IEPs, gender, too.

While differentiation offers teachers validation for attending to differences, on the surface it is neutral with regard to race and gender. The homogenous grouping that tends to occur with differentiation, RTI, and inclusion, however, clearly manifests along those lines. This is due in part to the framing of differentiation and inclusion in terms of individualistic models of social justice (Artiles, Harris-Murri, and Rostenberg 2006) that is buttressed by teachers' common wisdom on race and racial inequalities. To a large extent, however, this is also the result of teachers trying to be proficient in meeting the demands placed upon them. For example, if I am a teacher who has to spend a certain number of minutes every day with a group of RTI-Tier 2 students who are struggling with reading, then the most efficient way to utilize my time is to put those students in one reading group where I can do guided reading with all of them at the same time. Indeed, research has found that teachers often support tracking not because they think it might benefit students academically, but because they see it, as "a valuable tool to combat the awesome managerial challenges inherent in instructing large classes, often of diverse academic backgrounds, and the complexities of responding to individual student needs." (Ansalone and Biafora 2010: 3) Yet, because RTI-Tier 2 students, like IEP students, are overwhelming racial and ethnic minorities if I put these students together in one reading group in order to be "efficient," the reality is that this reading group is probably going to be mostly if not all nonwhite.

Further, the selection of groups and partners also reflects the ways that teachers do race (West and Fenstermaker 1995) in the classroom. After all, in a color-blind classroom where the problems of race are illusory, and disability as well, what difference does it make if students typically work in groups with other students of the same race and ability? I return to this question in chapter six when possible solutions for addressing inequality in schooling are considered. In the next chapter teachers' perspectives on gender in the classroom are explored.

Chapter Three

What Problem? Gender in the Gender-Blind Classroom

When I began the observation phase of this research, I thought I might see far more examples of "traditional" forms of racial as opposed to gender bias in the classroom. While I observed some examples of what I thought was blatant racial prejudice, for the most part, beliefs and behaviors regarding race played out at a more covert level in District 21. The displays of gender I observed in the classrooms, on the other hand, did not appear to have evolved much from the time of Barrie Thorne's influential work on gender and schooling in the early nineteen-nineties. In *Gender Play*, Thorne (1993) challenged the notion that boys and girls inhabit separate cultures and problematized both the common wisdom and scholarship that frames gender as dichotomous. The following examples from my field notes (almost twenty years later) also mirror many of Thorne's findings:

Field Notes: January 19, 2011, Fifth Grade General Education Class, Morgan Elementary

This morning Mr. Gira has transformed his classroom into Colonial Williamsburg for a social studies activity. Desks are grouped together in six stations representing the Governor's palace, the slave quarters, the shoemaker's shop, the tavern, the church, and the College of William and Mary and the dame school. He puts all the students into groups of two; all groups are same-gender except for one because there is an odd number of boys and girls who are present today.

As Mr. Gira explains to the students the activities they are expected to do at each station, he tells them when they get to the group of tables representing the college and the dame school, the girls have to do a "sewing" activity at the dame school, and the boys have to use a quill and paint to do a writing exercise at the college. Several boys laugh and a number of girls protest. One girl yells out, "But that's not fair!"

Mr. Gira tells her, "But this is Colonial Williamsburg and that's what women did, sew and take care of the home." This is the only station in this activity in which a strict interpretation of historical accuracy is enforced. At the slave quarters station, for example, white students are not instructed to behave as masters and minority students to behave as slaves.

Field Notes: October 5, 2010, Second Grade General Education Class, Morgan Elementary

As the students work on their assignment, I ask Ms. Parker why all of her reading groups are same-gender. Ms. Parker tells me that in her experience, girls are usually stronger readers than boys and although she has tried mixed-gender reading groups in the past, making the groups same-gender usually works better because girls in mixed-gender groups can sometimes "overpower" the boys.

Field Notes: October 25, 2010, Second Grade Dual Language Class, Helis Elementary

I arrive in Ms. Stevens' class at 9:30 a.m. after the students have returned from recess. A brief letter with grammatical errors is written on the board in Spanish and Ms. Lee, the co-teacher, is leading the students in making corrections. I record how many times children are called on by Ms. Lee in terms of gender: boy, boy, boy, boy, boy, boy, girl. Based on all my counts when I have observed Ms. Lee and Ms. Stevens directing lessons in this classroom, boys are consistently called on more often than girls, regardless of which students have their hands raised.

Field Notes: October 25, 2010, Third Grade General Education Class, Morgan Elemetary

Mr. Hamilton decides to break the students into three groups to work in science stations. The students are divided up into groups based on the colors of their clothing. Since the first color Mr. Hamilton calls is pink, every girl except for one ends up in the first group.

Mr. Hamilton, however, realized almost immediately that by not taking into account gender norms, he had unintentionally segregated his class by gender. In fact, Mr. Hamilton, an openly gay teacher at Morgan, was one of the most deliberately gender-conscious teachers with whom I worked. While it was common to see same-gender partners working together in his classroom, small groups were generally comprised of boys and girls. This was the exception rather than the rule.

Indeed, when I starting going into classrooms to observe, I was surprised to see how often teachers at all three schools allowed students to work in same-gender pairs and groups. I found this occurred for three main reasons. First, students almost always selected partners of the same gender when they were given the choice. Second, gender was often the variable teachers used to select partners and groups. Third, because the number of boys with Individualized Education Programs (IEPs) exceeded the number of girls, groups receiving special education services were generally same-gender.

Even though partners and small groups also tended to be homogenous in terms of race, the teachers in this study were far more concerned about racial inequality than gender inequality. As a result, the consequences of gender segregation did not appear to be problematic even though, as Thorne (1993) pointed out, when teachers gender segregate activities in their classrooms students pick up on and elaborate the oppositional and antagonistic meanings (67). I witnessed this on a few occasions when a boy and girl were paired together (most often because there was an odd number of boys and girls) and one or both expressed their disgust at having to work with someone of a different gender. As Benokraitis and Feagin pointed out in the mid-nineteen-eighties, when it comes to modern sexism, "Many of the battles won in the late 1960s and 1970s were limited or temporary victories." (1986: 25) Yet, unlike with racial discrimination, the general attitude among the teachers I worked with when it came to gender was that while enduring prejudices and support for traditional gender roles may still exist, in general, gender inequality and, in particular, institutional sexism, were not significant problems in schooling or society anymore.

Further, the environment of high-stakes testing associated with the No Child Left Behind Act of 2001 (NCLB) virtually assured that gender inequality would not be problematized in the near future in District 21. According to Nel Noddings, "The academic purpose of the school drives everything." (1992: 13) When test scores on the Illinois Standards Achievement Test (ISAT) are compared for boys and girls across all three schools in reading, science, and math, any differences between boys and girls, when they do exist, pale in comparison to differences found across racial groups. In addition, unlike with racial groups where whites score higher than Black and Hispanic students in every subject and in every grade, results when it comes to gender are less consistent; more fourth grade boys at Mason exceeded standards in reading than girls on the most recent ISAT while at Morgan, third, fourth, and fifth grade girls exceeded standards in math compared to boys. The bottom line is that as far as test scores in District 21 are concerned, gender is a non-issue (see also Noddings 2007). Interestingly, test scores on state report cards are not aggregated by sex *and* race.

In sum, I found teachers' perspectives on gender and sexism to be fundamentally different from their perspectives on race and racism. As a result, they were more likely to *deliberately* segregate students into groups based on gender, as opposed to unintentionally which was often the case with race; and unlike with race, teachers were inclined to believe that fundamental differences existed between boys and girls and those differences were most likely the result of biological, organic or natural phenomena. Indeed, while no teacher used the naturalization frame (Bonilla-Silva 2006) to explain the current status of racial minorities, it was the most common frame teachers used to buttress their understandings of gender and gender inequality as the following conversation between Mr. Foy and I one afternoon illustrates:

> LCS: Historically, gender inequality has been a significant problem in schooling. I'm curious to know if you think it's still a problem.
>
> Mr. Foy: No. I don't think it's a problem.
>
> [Silence]
>
> LCS: And can you expand on why you think it's not a problem?
>
> Mr. Foy: Well, I can only speak for my classroom. And I think that I give pretty much equal opportunities for all kids to learn. I don't base any of my educational decisions on gender. I do, however, have a tendency to group them mostly on gender because I find that the girls and the boys, um, maybe are more comfortable working in their own gender. Um, that's not always the case, but I do that frequently.

Interestingly in this exchange Mr. Foy denies that he takes into account gender when structuring his classroom, and in the next breath acknowledges that he frequently organizes groups according to gender. The contradictions of denying the significance of gender while at the same time essentializing it were a frequent occurrence in my interactions with teachers. In this chapter I highlight these contradictions as I explore teachers' use of the naturalization frame to explain the gender dynamics in their classrooms, their opposition to single-sex public schooling, and their repudiation of feminism.

GENDER-BLIND SEXISM AND THE NATURALIZATION CUL-DE-SAC

To be sure, viewing gender as a biological or "natural" phenomenon is not a new empirical finding. Indeed, according to Judith Lorber (1994), "Gender is so pervasive that in our society we assume it is bred into our genes." (13) To "do" gender, according to Candace West and Don Zimmerman (1986) is to create differences between men and women that are not natural or biological, yet once created reinforce the "essential" nature of gender (137). When I observed the teachers in this study do gender in the classroom, they often displayed what Benokraitis and Feagin (1986) referred to as accidental (or unintentional) dimensions of sex discrimination. For example, several teachers like Mr. Foy indicated the reason they allowed students to work in same-gender groups as often as they did was not because they thought boys and girls *should* be segregated in the classroom, but because the students preferred it, or the students were most comfortable working with others of the same gender. Teachers were not willing to validate this logic in regards to race.

Naturalization was not only reflected in teachers' perceptions about the comfort levels of students working in same-gender pairs and groups, but also in the policing of traditional gender role boundaries. In the following example, Ms. Stevens talks about her literature selections based on the gender composition of her second grade class:

> Well, I have like a really big group of boys in here. I just have a small amount of girls in here, and I find myself like at the library trying to find read-alouds that I think they're really going to enjoy. And, you know, I have to maybe not read *Fancy Nancy* and read *The Boy Who Loved Words* instead because you know that's more geared towards the students who are in here. Um, so I mean, I don't think as far as gender bias or inequalities or anything that there's any big issue.

Ms. Stevens' comments reveal another significant way in which teachers' treatment of gender differs from their treatment of race: despite its limitations, multiculturalism is viewed as an important vehicle in District 21 for bringing attention to the experiences of (racial) minorities in the context of a majority (white) institution. In Ms. Stevens' class girls were a noticeable minority in terms of both numbers and the attention they received, yet Ms. Stevens made it clear on more than one occasion that she was more concerned about attending to the preferences of the boys in her class rather than the girls. There is no equivalent of "multiculturalism" for addressing historical and contemporary sexism in District 21. Indeed, Women's History Month is not even celebrated in the schools where I observed.

A reliance on the naturalization frame was also reflected in teachers' perceptions of the academic potential and outcomes for boys and girls. In the following, Ms. Lee explains why she thinks more boys receive referrals for special education services than girls. Her response also typifies teachers' reluctance to acknowledge the pervasiveness of sexism:

> Ms. Lee: I still see it [gender] as an issue, um, not a problem.

LCS: Can you tell me what you mean by that?

Ms. Lee: It's [gender] noticeable. It's noticeable.

LCS: How so?

Ms. Lee: There's more boys that have IEPs in our building. There's more boys than girls hands down for sure. And that's always been the case. I don't know why. I tend more to believe that, you know, boys just, you know, take a little longer. They're a little more squirrely. But that's a generality for sure. (laughs) Um, and girls aren't. And they adapt I think a little more readily. Not all, again, but just as a general, you know, statement. But I don't see it as a problem...

Interestingly in our conversation, Ms. Lee acknowledges that by referring to boys as "squirrely" and girls as "easily adaptable" she is perpetuating stereotypical views of active boys and passive girls. Yet, she also legitimates this logic by situating it as the common wisdom that explains why more boys than girls are referred for special education services. The explanation for gendered outcomes is viewed as a consequence of the natural differences between boys and girls as opposed to the role teachers' perceptions of gender may play in making special education referrals.

Similar to Ms. Lee, Mr. Gira appealed to what he believed were inherent differences in boys and girls to support his claim that gender inequality was no longer a problem in schooling. In our discussion, he told me that girls now have all the opportunities that boys do and, in fact, he could count on the girls at the fifth grade level to be more hardworking and focused than the boys. When I asked why he thought this was, he replied:

I think they [girls] mature faster and boys are still little boys in fifth grade. They're not really very mature but girls start to mature a little earlier and just the nature of their personality. They're more sedentary, they can focus, you know, they're not as active and moving around as much as boys. Um, I mean, rarely do I have problems with girls in that area. Whereas boys are just, they have too much energy and it shows in school.

Whereas Ms. Lee used the term "easily adaptable" to describe girls in the classroom and "squirrely" to describe boys, Mr. Gira describes girls as "sedentary" and boys as "immature." This logic not only reinforces the notion that boys and girls are hardwired differently; it also suggests that if there is any gender-related problem in schooling today, the problem resides with boys and not girls. Indeed, a number of scholars and activists share Ms. Lee's and Mr. Gira's beliefs about the dynamics of gender in the classroom, claiming that girls as opposed to boys are "model students" who have successfully triumphed over their historical educational disadvantages; if gender inequality exists at all today, it is boys who are losing out, not girls (e.g., Newkirk 2002/2000; Sommers 2002/2000). In fact, most teachers in this study also concurred with Ms. Lee's and Mr. Gira's assessment of contemporary gender inequality: the pendulum had swung too far in the opposite direction, towards girls and away from boys. Unfortunately, an important consequence of the assumption that girls are "model" students and are no longer collectively disadvantaged is that girls may not be seen as deserving of particular attention or educational resources (Archer, Halsall, and Hollingworth 2007; Williams, Jamieson and Hollingworth 2008; see also Lent and Figueira-McDonough 2002; Saunders et al. 2004; Crosnoe, Riegle-Crumb, and Muller 2007).

In the end, the belief that boys and girls are fundamentally different was perhaps nowhere more insidious than in teachers' opinions of single-sex public schooling. Interestingly, the logic on which the social equality maxim is predicated would suggest that teachers reject the notion of single-sex schooling on the same grounds most rejected ACC: no group should be singled out for "special treatment." In reality, the majority of teachers *were* opposed to the idea of single-sex public schooling at the elementary level, but were willing to consider formal segregation of boys and girls beginning in middle school, at least for some portion of the school day. Their reasoning once again was consonant with the logic of naturalization.

TEACHERS' PERSPECTIVES ON SINGLE-SEX SCHOOLING

While multiculturalism continues to be offered as a solution for enduring racial inequality in schooling, one solution for addressing gender inequality that has gained some momentum in recent years is a return to single-sex public schooling. According to the National Association for Single Sex Public Education (2011) there are currently 524 public schools in the United States offering single-sex programming, of which 103 operate exclusively as either an all-girl school or all-boy school. This number is expected to increase in the future; in fact, some states like South Carolina have made single-sex programming the cornerstone of their educational policy with ninety-seven schools in the state embracing single-sex options in an effort to boost public school choice and test scores (McNeil 2008). Meghan Carr (2007) argues that support for single-sex schooling usually falls into one of three categories: the first and most controversial is that boys and girls are hardwired differently and therefore learn differently; the second argument reflects the neoliberal perspective that parents should have diverse options when it comes to educating their children; and the third argument concerns social interactions in the classroom between boys and girls which include distractions related to members of the opposite sex and differences in how boys and girls may be treated in coeducational settings. It is important to note the logic implied in the last argument does not take into account sexual orientation (Smith 1998).

After observing the pervasiveness of gender segregation in all three schools, I decided to ask teachers about their perspectives on single-sex public schooling. In general, the teachers in this study were opposed to single-sex public elementary schools because it violated two basic corollaries of the social equality maxim: (1) the school as a microcosm of society must teach girls and boys to work with one another: social location is inconsequential therefore there is no purpose in educating boys and girls separately; and (2) boys and girls when educated together contribute something unique to the learning environment. The explanation teachers offered in support of the second corollary underscores their beliefs in the inherent differences between boys and girls. Indeed, according to Thorne (1993), "The separate-and-different-worlds story is seductive. It gives full weight to the fact that girls and boys often *do* separate in daily interactions, especially when they create more lasting groups and friendships." (90) Interestingly, in the following conversation between Ms. Stevens and me, she appeals to the separate cultures argument to oppose single-sex schooling.

> LCS: Recently, some parents and educators have advocated for a return to single-sex public education, and NLCB made available $3 million dollars in grant money to experiment with such options. As a teacher, do you think this is a good way to address issues associated with gender in schooling?
>
> Ms. Stevens: I don't think that's a good idea only because I think they [students] learn so much from each other and just the attributes of like boys and girls are so different in a classroom. I mean, like they teach each other such valuable lessons during the day and also that's just not like how society, it's just not how it is.

While the teachers I worked with generally rejected the idea of public single-sex elementary schools, several were willing to concede possible benefits of segregating schools or programming on the basis of gender at the middle or high school level. The logic teachers used to support this argument was particularly insightful; the underlying assumption was that while gender inequality was not a major problem in elementary school, it potentially became a problem after fifth grade. As Ms. Lopez argued, "Something happens at puberty. Ten is almost like a magical age for girls. They're still confident; they're still equal with boys in some ways, and something happens where then they all of a sudden-they become girls, you know."

According to C.J. Pascoe, "The ordering of sexuality from elementary school through high school is inseparable from the institutional ordering of gendered identities." (2007: 26-27) While none of the teachers specifically talked about "sexuality" in discussing single-sex schooling, the justifications they often gave in support of sex segregation included behavioral distractions and problems that emerged when boys and girls were educated together. In the following, Ms. Smith talks about why she supports single-sex public schooling:

> Ms. Smith: I wrote a master's thesis on that [single-sex schooling]. Um, I think that we would have a lot less issues.
>
> LCS: What kinds of issues would single-sex schooling solve?
>
> Ms. Smith: I think kind of the behavior issues and the need to kind of show off. Um, and impress and the worry about how, how we're dressed which is, is such an issue that it causes inequity, um, in, in the classroom. The kids are very concerned about—like Abby is always, you know, you know, (makes motions to indicate well-dressed) and, and the other girls are like (makes motions to indicate not as well-dressed), you know, and boys will like her [Abby] better than, and, and it's that kind of thing that it's very, it's like we're not focusing on the learning, so yeah. So I think that would make a difference and also take a lot of pressure off her [Abby].
>
> LCS: So you support single-sex schooling from kindergarten through twelfth grade?
>
> Ms. Smith: Yeah. Oh, yeah.

Note the heteronormativity implicit in Ms. Smith's logic: separating boys and girls in schooling in order to avoid sexual distractions assumes the heterosexuality of boys and girls. What is also insightful about the conversations I had with teachers about single-sex schooling is they reveal not only a belief in the asexuality of students until at least grade five, but a belief that gender-related problems if they exist do not generally begin until that time. Then, when problems do occur one possible solution is to segregate boys and girls in the classroom as opposed to addressing male privilege and heteronormativity.

Teachers' perspectives on single-sex schooling complicate our understanding of gender equality in a number of important ways. Indeed, whether in favor of single-sex public schooling or opposed, as most were, every teacher grounded his or her perspective in an appeal to "equality." Yet, in both cases, the appeal to equality was based on a notion of equity rooted in abstract liberalism (Bonilla-Silva 2006), underpinned by an essentialist logic predicated on the belief that the reason boys and girls should learn together, or *not*, was because the inherent differences between them created a unique learning environment, whether beneficial *or* problematic. Further, for teachers' who supported some form of single-sex schooling past grade five their responses underscored again the belief that gender discrimination was individualistic in nature; it was something that happened to *individual* girls and *individual* boys due to the distractions caused by the opposite sex. In the end, while an appeal to equality was made by every teacher, it was an understanding of equality in which institutional sexism and heteronormativity were unaccounted for and therefore unattended. This logic also informed teachers' beliefs about feminism.

THE "F" WORD

When I asked Ms. Jackson, a fifth grade general education teacher at Helis, one day over lunch whether she considered herself a feminist teacher, she laughed. When I then asked her why she was amused by that question, she told me the terminology, "feminist," seemed so outdated. Feminism, the fight for gender equality, was simply not needed at this point in history, she argued, which makes the conversation that followed those remarks all the more interesting:

> Ms. Jackson: I think there's more choices for women [today]. I mean, I have an aunt who has a Ph.D. She was the Chair of the English department at Midwestern University and she did that because she wanted to and she could. And then later in life had her children at 45. And wishes that she had her kids, um, earlier cause she wishes she had time to have more, but she had to put her kids aside to do [that]. I made a choice to stay home with my kids. It was the best thing I ever did and I wouldn't trade it for the world. I have a little one now so in some ways like I remember when I chose not to return to work I felt like oh, no, people are going to say that I am forsaking my career for my children. Instead of "you should stay home" it was "you should stay at work." And then when I went back to work I had this feeling of oh, my god, I'm forsaking our child and are people going to judge me for going back to work?

> LCS: Sounds like a lot of pressure.

> Ms. Jackson: There is pressure. I think there is pressure, that is true. For the woman to juggle career and children. And to feel like you're meeting your own, you know? So I think that there's a lot of like assumptions, but I think there's more of a like broader choice going on then what I recall as a child.

This conversation between Ms. Jackson and me offers a number of powerful insights once again into how social inequalities are viewed in an era of post-racial and post-gendered politics. Ms. Jackson's argument that gender inequality is no longer a problem is based on her assessment that women have more *choices* today than they did in the past. As she continues, however, it becomes clear that neither of the choices she offers as examples have necessarily positive outcomes for the women who choose them. Further, there is no discussion of *why* it is her aunt with the Ph.D. might have had to forgo having children until later in life because of the demands of academia or why Ms. Jackson struggled to choose between going back to work after her youngest child was born or staying home full-time because of the pressure she felt would inevitably result from either decision. Yet, this is the same teacher who only moments earlier told me that feminism was superfluous because the battle for gender equality had been won decades earlier.

In general, teachers' attitudes towards feminism offered another important example of the differences between their perspectives on race and gender. Just as teachers thought of race and gender as two distinct entities, they viewed antiracism and feminism as almost polar opposites. For example, when asked, every teacher to some degree wanted to be considered an antiracist teacher; at the very least, this was considered a noble ambition. There were few teachers, however, who accepted the title "feminist teacher." Indeed, it was often the same teachers who embraced the label of antiracist teacher that fervently rejected the label of feminist teacher. Further, among those teachers who did consider themselves feminists, even if halfheartedly, they aligned themselves with liberal feminism.

Anticipating teachers may be uncomfortable talking about feminism given the widespread efforts to dismantle the women's movement and feminist platforms beginning in the late 1970s (Douglas and Michaels 2004), I broached the topic by first asking teachers about gender inequality. Then, when teachers asserted favorable attitudes towards gender equality, as all did in this study, I asked whether they considered themselves feminist teachers. In the end, I was surprised by how fundamentally different teachers' reactions to feminism were compared to antiracism. My expectation was that teachers committed to feminism would also be committed to antiracism and vice versa. However, a number of self-described antiracist teachers immediately rejected the idea they were feminists.

On the one hand, this is a matter of semantics. After all, what teacher would want to be considered an *anti*-antiracist teacher? Certainly, in today's society one would expect far less stigma for identifying as "antiracist" as opposed to "feminist." Further, although teachers were reluctant to identify themselves as feminists, they nonetheless expressed support for a number of mainstream feminist goals. The brand of equality on which these platforms are based, however, is synonymous with liberal feminism. Rejecting "feminism" and supporting "antiracism" therefore is not *just* a matter of semantics. "Feminism" for most of the teachers in this study was understood to be *favoring* girls over boys, as opposed to "antiracism" which was perceived as treating *everyone* fairly regardless of race.

Indeed, when I asked Ms. Mendez, a first grade dual language teacher at Morgan Elementary, whether she considered herself a feminist teacher the question she posed back to me was, "Feminist in the sense that I think women are better?" Similarly, when I asked Mr. Gold, a fourth grade teacher at Morgan, the same question, he responded:

> A feminist teacher? No. I just consider myself a teacher. I don't, I don't think I, uh, you know, favor one group over another in any way. I don't think any student should come home 'oh, my teacher, put down this group or that group,' so I try very hard to keep my politics out of school, to not make any child feel like, you know, the teacher is against them.

In fact, even the few teachers who considered themselves feminists were careful to point out they were just as concerned about boys' success as they were girls':

> LCS: Do you consider yourself a feminist teacher?

> Ms. Hurley: Oh, probably. Probably. But I'm also, I feel like I'm also an advocate for, you know, so much of the time, Black males are maligned, you know. And, and we have to understand that, um, cultural differences and class differences, um, play a major role in how they see themselves. You know, they don't see themselves necessarily as having, some boys, you know, whether they're Latino or they're Black mostly, they don't see themselves with a lot of aspirations, you know. I want them to have dreams. Dreams that I keep telling them are achievable; I see you have this gift.

In the end, "feminism" was seen as running counter to abstract liberal (Bonilla-Silva 2006) claims to equality whereas antiracism was seen as logically compatible. Not surprisingly, teacher's rejected the notion that feminism played an important role in their approach to teaching. As Ms. Lee, a second and third grade inclusion teacher at Helis Elementary told me, "I mean, I firmly believe in all of the feminist, um, values and—not values, um, their stances, you know, their platforms. I do believe in them, but I wouldn't say that that drives my instruction or that's my philosophy of teaching."

According to Allen Johnson (2005), "If feminism is invisible, patriarchy is invisible. And if feminism is distorted and discredited, patriarchy is safe from scrutiny, for feminism is the only critical perspective on patriarchy we've got." (191) To speak of feminism in many ways is a misnomer; indeed, there are many types of feminisms. While Shira Tarrant (2006) warns that an emphasis on distinguishing between feminist traditions, while useful and necessary at times, often leads to viewing these traditions as oppositional and therefore irreconcilable, it is also important to consider the contributions and limitations of particular agendas, and if any brand of feminism was deemed acceptable by the teachers I worked with it was liberal feminism. Indeed, when it comes to education, liberal feminists have done much to make the playing field more level for women and girls (Tong 1998). In addition to providing a platform for the passage of Title IX, the liberal feminist agenda for addressing inequality in schooling includes increasing opportunities for girls and women in underrepresented areas like math, science, and sports, and providing a legal framework for challenging discrimination such as sexual harassment.

Liberal feminism, however, also has a number of fundamental shortcomings. First, the measure of equality that emerges from the liberal feminist agenda is clearly based on the position of men; if masculinity is privileged then in order to advance gender equality girls and women must be *raised* to the level of boys and men by removing legal and political obstacles that bar access. The liberal feminist framework for addressing gender discrimination in schooling problematizes male privilege only to the extent that it does not entitle women to the same spoils attached to masculinity. As Barbara Katz Rothman argued in 1989, "The liberal feminists, in asking that the ladies be remembered, are not so much offering a critique of American life and values as they are seeking full access." (194) In this way, it becomes inconceivable to ask whether boys should be compared or *raised* to the level of girls since it is femininity, not masculinity that must be "overcome."

Indeed, it is even possible for the liberal feminist agenda to *create* obstacles to obtaining gender equality in schooling given the current climate of high-stakes testing. First, if masculinity serves as the ideal type and girls begin to outpace boys as they have in areas like reading and writing, then not only are antifeminists inclined to believe that gender inequality has been alleviated but that perhaps the pendulum has swung too far in the opposite direction as evidenced by the aforementioned debates about the existence of a "boy crisis" in public schooling (e.g., Newkirk 2002/2000; Sommers 2002/2000; Rivers and Barnett 2006; Okopny 2008). Second, as long as gender equality is measured exclusively in terms of test scores and the ability of girls to gain access to coursework and disciplines historically underrepresented by women then other manifestations of sexism can easily go unattended.

Further, in the case of liberal feminism, the patriarchal structure of society in which public schooling not only functions but serves as a vehicle to legitimate male dominance and heteronormativity (and, of course, white privilege as well) goes unchallenged. According to Johnson (2005), liberal feminism relegates male privilege to an individual problem disconnected from the larger social structure that promotes it: "A basic problem with liberal feminism (and liberalism in general) is that its intense focus on the individual obscures the power of social systems. This is one reason why liberal feminism doesn't recognize patriarchy as something to be reckoned with." (115) Not surprisingly, liberal feminism is the most palatable form of feminism in the U.S., and whether teachers wanted to call themselves feminists or not, every teacher I worked with voiced a commitment to the basic tenets of the liberal feminist platform. Indeed, it is a platform consonant with the social equality maxim: all children, boys and girls alike, have the same potential for academic success. How then did teachers account for what they viewed as subtle and fundamental differences between the boys and girls in their classes? Again, the logic of naturalization offered what appeared to be a sound explanation.

A NOTE ON SEXUALITY

While I was particularly attuned to recording how teachers performed gender and race in the classroom, I was also very deliberate from the moment I entered the field about discerning any instances in which sexuality was particularly salient in the classroom (see for example Cahill and Adams 1997; Smith 1998; Lasser and Tharinger 2003; Lindsay, Perlesz, Brown, McNair, de Vaus, and Pitts 2006). However, I found very few instances in which I had the opportunity to *dynamically center* sexuality (Collins 2008). Indeed, it was extremely rare that "sexuality" even came up in my conversations with teachers. The two exceptions involve a second grader at Morgan whose mothers are lesbians and my work with Mr. Hamilton. I am reluctant to make any claims about heterosexism or homophobia in schooling based on this limited data, however, it does suggest some interesting questions for future research.

In order to create a sense of security and to build community in their classrooms, the teachers I observed, particularly in the lower grades, would often ask students to bring in a picture of their family to put up in the classroom. It was not unusual for teachers like Ms. Parker to go a step farther and have the students share stories about their family with the other students, an activity that younger students especially seemed to enjoy. For the first time this school year, Ms. Parker had a student bring in a picture of himself with his two mothers and sisters. Ms. Parker embraced the added diversity this brought to her class, but was also sensitive about making sure her student felt safe to talk about his family:

> LCS: Did your students enjoy sharing information about themselves with the class about their families?
>
> Ms. Parker: They loved it! They loved hearing about each other's families. And I have one student who comes from a same-sex household, didn't it, nobody (makes motion to indicate the other students could have cared less)
>
> LCS: The kids were like 'eh?' (shrugs shoulders indicating no big deal)
>
> Ms. Parker: Exactly. Exactly. Which I think is fabulous in contrast to how kids might have reacted when I was their age.
>
> LCS: I find that refreshing.

Ms. Parker: Yeah. I had made sure prior to his sharing, though, that I read a picture book which wasn't so to the point, but it was—it's about these two hens who fight over this one egg and then at the end of the book, the, uh, the text is something like this chick was the luckiest chick in the world because it now has two moms who love and care about him. And I just wanted them to hear that about—the plot wasn't about that at all. It's this great story of a weasel and the egg and it's fantastic, but I thought, well, I'll just, you know, slide that in. Um, so I think that's definitely a way then hopefully to foster that feeling of safety is starting from a place of I want to hear about your family, and I accept you and your family and I think by my model hopefully they'll feel that and act on that as well.

This incident begs the question: what might a sexuality-blind classroom look like, taking into account the current dynamics of the color- and gender-blind classroom? If Ms. Parker's model serves as the benchmark for the treatment of sexuality, then it will most likely reflect an interesting cooptation of the current approach to dealing with race and gender in District 21. While it is unlikely that sexuality will be addressed in the same fashion as Hispanic Heritage month, for example, incorporating literature about gays and lesbians or written by gay and lesbian authors, as is often the approach when it comes to race, would appear to compliment District 21's current practice of multiculturalism. However, it also seems likely given the inextricable link between gender and sexuality that sexuality will be treated in some respects like gender: invisible, a non-problem. Yet, unlike with both race and gender, it is doubtful that sexuality would serve as a vehicle to segregate partners and small groups at the elementary school level. Regardless, I cannot fathom District 21's treatment of sexuality including a systematic critique of heterosexism and homophobia based on what I observed in terms of their approach to racial and gender inequality. These, however, are important considerations for future research especially in this era of heightened attention to school bullying and the victimization of gay and lesbian students (Thurlow 2001; Bontempo and D'Augelli 2002; Lasser and Tharinger 2003).

A second important consideration for future research in this area is whether openly gay and lesbian teachers challenge the heteronormativity endemic to the institution of education in the U.S. or whether the countervailing effects of privilege, ruling relations, and structural constraints lead gay and lesbian teachers to promote homonormativity (Duggan 2002). Mr. Hamilton offers an excellent case in point. One of the first things I noticed when I entered Mr. Hamilton's third grade classroom was the picture of him and his husband on his desk. In my observations, I also found it was common for students to ask Mr. Hamilton questions about his husband just as students would often ask questions about the families of straight teachers. For example, the Monday following Halloween a girl in Mr. Hamilton's class asked what costumes he and his husband had worn in a tone and demeanor that indicated there was nothing peculiar about this question in the least. Mr. Hamilton would also use personal examples in class that referred to his spouse.

I looked forward to the opportunity to ask Mr. Hamilton about his experience of being an openly gay teacher in District 21 and finally one afternoon had an opportunity to join him and his class on the playground. I asked Mr. Hamilton if he had ever received any flak from teachers, administrators, or parents for being openly gay. Mr. Hamilton told me that no one had complained to his face, but that regardless he would not have it any other way; according to Mr. Hamilton, it was imperative that he be true to himself.

Interestingly, Mr. Hamilton remarked on a couple of occasions that he believed his social location as a gay male teacher offered him unique insights into gender; indeed, he was the only teacher whom I worked with who believed that gender inequality was still a significant problem in schooling and in society. In the following, Mr. Hamilton offers his understanding of the social construction of gender and the ways in which schooling tends to promote essentialism:

> I think there's two huge things that happen at schools. First, is that people assume there are differences between boys and girls that don't exist. Um, there just is no—and I, I'm an evidence person. I like to know what I am talking about, and I am happy to be challenged, persuaded if I'm, if I'm wrong, you know. Um, but there just—why is it that boys seem to be playing football more? Is it because it really is a spatial thing happening or is it because people are tossing footballs at boys when they're young, and not tossing footballs at girls when they're young? Um, I, I tend to think it's because of what we're explicitly teaching and the, and the connections that are firing inside a person's head happen because of the experiences that we have.

While Mr. Hamilton acknowledges the polarization of gender that has long underscored research on boys and girls in schooling (e.g., Thorne 1993; Campbell and Wahl 2002/1998), and was more willing than other teachers I worked with to believe gender was socially constructed, I found his approach and demeanor in the classroom generally reflected a more homonormative standpoint. Homonormativity refers to a political stance taken by gays and lesbians that espouses support for dominant heteronormative assumptions and institutions (Duggan 2002: 179). Homonormativity, according to Susan Stryker (2008), is not only a macropolitical extension of neoliberalism, but a micropolitical force that maintains dominant constructions of knowledge, power, and authority. While Mr. Hamilton's ideas about gender appear more progressive than the other teachers in this study, he generally placed more emphasis on data-driven approaches to schooling and the importance of internalizing school culture than his colleagues. I suggest, therefore, that future institutional ethnographies specifically explore the relationship between teachers' sexuality, hetero- and homonormativity, and privilege in the current climate of post-racial and post-gendered politics.

CONCLUSION

In *Race in the Schoolyard* (2005), Amanda Lewis discusses the challenges of trying to study race in a predominantly white school where educators, parents, and students did not consider race to be a "problem" since white people did not think of themselves as *raced* and there were so few racial minority students who attended the school (see also Lewis 1994). Lewis' frustrations of trying to problematize something that participants did not see as a problem kept coming to mind as I attempted to study attitudes about gender and gender-related behaviors at Morgan, Mason, and Helis. For the most part, the sentiment among teachers I talked to was that gender inequality was not a major problem in today's society. Yet, there were clear examples in my field notes of behaviors and attitudes that had not changed much over the years. In fact, some teachers who dismissed the notion that institutional sexism was a problem, began to realize once they started to share some of the behaviors they had observed in their classrooms that perhaps there *was* still more work to be done. Ms. Smith was one of those teachers. The following is a conversation she and I had in the hallway outside her classroom one afternoon:

> Ms. Smith: Um, I, I teach a Math Olympiad class in the morning, and, um, it's, it's interesting…. It's interesting, um, because the boys are much more willing to take risks in math than the girls. It's been kind of an eye-opening experience to see how the boys are like, they'll just dive in and, and take risks and shout out answers, and the girls are still very, you know, "can you help me?"
>
> LCS: What age group are we talking about here?
>
> Ms. Smith: Fourth and fifth grade. And so, yeah, that shows me that, that there still is a lot of inequity in, at least in the lower grades of how math is taught and how it's approached, um, same with science. Same with science. Yeah, I do see that in science even though it's very hands-on in this district. The girls are much less willing to be leaders during science.

I also had an opportunity to observe part of a Math Olympiad meeting after school at Morgan where there was one girl present out of approximately twenty boys. Since Mr. Gira was a faculty sponsor I asked him about the gender ratio of Math Olympiad and he confirmed that historically there have been three times as many boys than girls participate.

Ms. Smith's colleague at Mason, Mr. Swain, observed a similar pattern among his third grade students when it came to math and science, but interpreted these dynamics as fairly inconsequential since girls generally out-paced boys in reading in his class:

> I tend to notice that the boys are more into the math and science, um, as in the traditional argument. Maybe not as much, but I do think in general for the most part, um, that's an area that, um, you just don't see as much representation from the girls. And it's, but it's the opposite in reading. Um, I think girls, the girls that I've had in class tend to do, or perform much better with reading then, uh, the boys do. But, yeah, beyond that, um, I don't really sense, um, too much of an inequality.

According to Barbara Risman (1999), "Gender expectations are socially constructed and sustained by socialization, interactional expectations, and institutional arrangements." (152) What do these contemporary examples of girls' participation in math and science in a *socially progressive* community suggest about socialization, expectations, and institutional arrangements in District 21? Further, in what ways might the construction of color- and gender-blind classrooms serve to perpetuate the tracking of boys and girls into certain academic interest areas based upon gender stereotypes of *squirrely boys* and *sedentary girls*? After all, the color- and gender-blind classroom share many things in common. Indeed, as manifestations of the social equality maxim they are both predicated on the beliefs that social location does not matter; all students have access to the same opportunities for success; and any prejudice or discrimination that occurs in today's society resides not in social institutions but individual bigots.

Yet, there are also stark differences between how teachers construct the color- and gender-blind classroom because their beliefs about race and gender as markers of identity are fundamentally different. With the exception of Mr. Hamilton, most teachers in this study viewed gender unlike race as a matter of essential difference. This allowed teachers to denounce gender inequality all the while holding to the belief that boys and girls are inherently different whether due to biology or some other natural phenomena. Teachers might therefore acknowledge stereotypical behaviors in their classrooms when they occurred, but still chalk them up to a matter of "girls-will-be-girls" and "boys-will-be-boys." This was not the case with race; if anything teachers went out of their way to avoid such language in speaking about race and race-related issues. Here, the sentiment was "we are all the same" even though their attitudes and behaviors tended to reflect the logic of color-blind racism.

In conclusion, while teachers' attitudes towards race and gender are different in many respects, the denial of *institutional* racism and sexism virtually assures the perpetuation of both. As Judith Lorber (1994) argues, "Gender has changed in the past and will change in the future, but without deliberate restructuring it will not necessarily change in the direction of greater equality between men and women." (6) Addressing racism and sexism at an individu-al-level may be necessary but it is not sufficient for alleviating structural inequalities. Indeed, focusing only on *individuals* further obscures the ruling relations in which teachers participate on a daily basis. It is this system of ruling relations that I explore in detail in the next chapter, but first I return to Colonial Williamsburg.

RETURNING TO COLONIAL WILLIAMSBURG

I began this chapter with a vignette about a fifth grade social studies exercise taken from my field notes. When I returned to Mr. Gira's class a few days after the Colonial Williamsburg exercise took place, he was preparing to review the lesson and give the students a quiz over the material. To be fair, turning the classroom into a modest representation of Colonial Williamsburg was not Mr. Gira's idea; it was part of the standard social studies curriculum adopted by District 21. Mr. Gira, however, as the teacher has a lot of autono-my in what he chooses to emphasize about the lesson, what additional infor-mation he offers to share, and how he responds to students' questions.

Mr. Gira begins the review by asking the students what they remember about the exercise.

A white girl calls out, "Some people were not treated as well as other people!"

"Okay," Mr. Gira says. "Who weren't treated as well?"

Several students shout out, "The slaves!" No one makes reference to women being treated as second-class citizens.

Mr. Gira concurs. "Yeah, the slaves were pretty much mistreated." A gross understatement, in my opinion. Mr. Gira goes on to ask, "Why was slavery necessary during this time?"

I can think of myriad ways in which this conversation with the students would allow Mr. Gira to address issues of white privilege, power, racism, how slaves and women were not considered fully human under the law, how neither had access to the full rights of citizenship, and the contemporary parallels that could be drawn, but he does none of this. Instead he makes the comment, "African Americans did a lot of things for us to make this country great that no one else was willing to do." There was a choice in the matter?

Mr. Gira uses his curriculum guide to go over each station that was part of the original exercise. When he gets to the College of William and Mary and the dame school, he asks the students how education was different in Colonial Williamsburg than it is now.

A white girl responds, "Some girls didn't go to school!"

"And if they did," Mr. Gira says, "they had to learn to sew and take care of the home because that was their job." Again, an opportunity to talk about patriarchy and women's subordination is lost.

Mr. Gira asks the students what the purpose of the tavern was and several kids shout out answers: to talk politics, to play games, to visit. There is no mention of the fact that these were essentially white men's spaces. Indeed, Mr. Gira tells them the tavern was a place everyone could go.

A white girl raises her hand, confused, and asks, "Were Black people allowed in the tavern?"

"No, slaves were not allowed in the tavern," Mr. Gira says.

"That's not very fair!" she protests.

Mr. Gira agrees and then asks the students to talk about the slaves and how they were treated. He attempts to express the inhumanity of slavery, but this sentiment is lost when he makes statements like, "Some slaves worked in the masters' houses and those were pretty good jobs."

A white boy, looking perplexed, asks, "Well, since there would have been more slaves than white people on a plantation, why didn't they rebel? Why did they stay enslaved?"

Mr. Gira tries to articulate the fear that whites instilled in slaves and the consequences of rebellion, but there is no condemnation of the immorality of slavery, nor is there condemnation of women's second class status in Colonial Williamsburg.

In my classroom observations at all three schools, Mr. Gira's treatment of race and gender is not unique. The teachers I worked with were aware that social inequalities existed although they believed that some like racism were far more acute than others like sexism. Teachers' resistance to address inequalities as contemporary, ongoing, structural problems, not historical phenomena or manifestations of individual-level bigotries, however were consistently undermined by the ruling relations in District 21 and the countervailing effects of privilege including teachers' own privilege, the (white) privilege of their students and their students' families, and the privilege associated with Lakeview. All three types of privilege are examined in detail in chapter five. In order to provide a context for this exegesis of privilege, however, the organizational complexes in which the teachers participate on a daily basis must first be understood. In the next chapter, I map the ruling relations that govern the institutions and therefore the day-to-day interactions in which the teachers participate.

Chapter Four

Mapping the Ruling Relations

Critics are so intent on exposing the racism and obtuseness of the teacher that it is difficult to understand her [sic] view of the world. Like welfare workers and police, teachers in the urban colonies of the poor are part of a social system that shares *their* behavior, too. It is more important to expose and correct the injustice of the social system than to scold its agents. Indeed, one of the chief reasons for the failures of educational reforms of the past has been precisely that they called for a change of philosophy or tactics on the part of the individual school employee rather than system change-and concurrent transformations in the distribution of power and wealth in the society as a whole. (Tyack 1974: 10-11)

In chapters two and three, I illustrated some of the ways that teachers talk about race and gender in an era of post-racial and post-gendered politics. I also offered some examples of how teachers *do* race and gender in the context of color- and gender-blind classrooms. This is not, however, where the story begins and ends, a simple tale of prejudicial teachers in need of "diversity" or "sensitivity" training. This is a story about teachers working in an environment that reinforces and rewards the color- and gender-blind logic many have chosen to adopt and offers no incentive for those who have not to rock the boat. To tell this complicated story requires mapping the ruling relations (Smith 1990; 2005).

By mapping the ruling relations we can observe the ways teachers' agency is both constrained and enabled by the organizational complexes they encounter in their everyday lives. The map allows us to explore, for example, the ways the institutions in which the teachers participate systematically work against the probability that teachers will take the risk of publicly acknowledging and addressing institutional racism and sexism. Through interviews and observations of the teachers in this study and the analysis of texts, a map of ruling relations crystallized, providing an institutional context for understanding teachers' attitudes and behaviors towards race and gender revealed in chapters two and three (Figure 4.1).

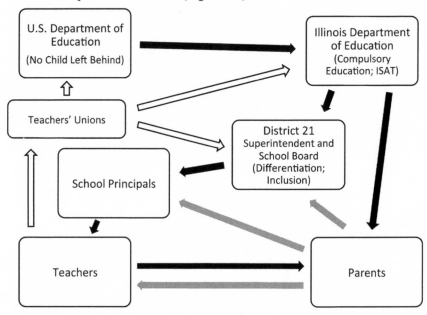

Figure 4.1.

In Figure 4.1, the arrows identify the ruling relations that govern the organizational complexes in which the teachers in this study participate and provide a visual representation of the institutionalization of educational policies such as the No Child Left Behind Act of 2001 (NCLB). For example, the U.S. Department of Education is charged with ensuring that school districts comply with NCLB or face mandated penalties. The Illinois Department of Education adopts the Illinois Standards Achievement Test (ISAT) as the means to measure whether each public school in Illinois is making adequate yearly progress (AYP) and thus in compliance with NCLB. To ensure that all its schools meet AYP, District 21 adopts policies such as differentiation and RTI in an attempt to increase students' academic success. Principals of schools within the district bear the responsibility of making sure their teachers are effectively implementing District 21 policies and preparing students to succeed on the ISATs. Finally, teachers, under pressure to produce students who pass the ISATs or face consequences including negative outcomes on their performance evaluations, rely on parents to read with their children, feed their children breakfast before coming to school, and to make sure their children have completed their homework.

Given the teachers' positions within the ruling relations of District 21, essentially one rung above parents within the formal hierarchy of authority, it is no surprise that teachers' explanations for the success or failure of their students rests heavily with parents. In reality, teachers are often made the scapegoats when students underperform; the common wisdom is that if teachers are doing their jobs effectively, then students should be making academic gains (see for example Ingersoll 2005). Well aware of this argument especially in an era of high-stakes testing, teachers in this study generally turned the tables, making parents the scapegoats. This was essentially based on the same argument; if parents are doing their jobs effectively then students should be able to perform well in school. As Mr. Swain told me one afternoon, "Politicians, you know, speak about teachers…but so much of it is what the kids bring from home, you know, from a very young age because if the parents give it to them it's easier at school, you know."

It did not take long once I started spending time in classrooms to become intimately acquainted with teachers' positions within the ruling relations of the school district, and I would argue the educational system in general. The following is a conversation Ms. Hurley and I had one morning after her students went to art. As soon as the students left that morning, I could tell Ms. Hurley wanted to bend my ear. This was not uncommon in my interactions with teachers as many were happy to have someone to listen to what they had to say about their daily challenges.

Once the students left for art class, Ms. Hurley turned to me and said, "You know last week you were asking me about equity. I want to clarify more of what I meant by my response."

Ms. Hurley reminded me of her complaints last week about the time she is now expected to devote to writing out lesson plans. According to Ms. Hurley, District 21 recently hired a nationally known "lesson plan expert," Wendy Jackson. Ms. Hurley made clear that the problem, however, was not Wendy. In fact, she talked to Wendy who stated that the superintendent and the school board had misinterpreted her expectations. Wendy realized that it was impossible for teachers to do what they needed to do in the classroom (and outside) if they were regularly spending several hours producing written, detailed lesson plans.

I asked if teachers at every school in District 21 had to comply with the new lesson plan dictate. Ms. Hurley told me they do, however, the principals have the discretion as to how this is carried out. At some schools, she told me teachers do the task together, perhaps once a month. It appeared the expectation at Mason was that lesson plans be done far more frequently. I wondered if this was because Mason was not a top-performing school.

"The problem," Ms. Hurley informed me, "is that the superintendent is a politician, not an educator. And the board is not made up of educators. They don't realize the challenges we have here in the classroom. They don't know what it's like when a teacher can't get a young girl to concentrate because she was raped yesterday. They don't know what it's like when they put all the demands on us and the parents don't care."

She made a reference to the upcoming documentary *Waiting for Superman.* "I won't even see that. Just seeing the previews makes me so angry. Charter schools have lots of problems as well. Some work, but many do not. And the major difference with charter schools is that the parents *want* their children to go to those schools. Those children understand the importance their parents are putting on education and the benefits of attending that school. Here, the school is just open to whoever lives within the school boundaries. So you have parents who drop their kids off at 7:45 in the morning—the school doesn't open until 9:00! Their parents won't even try to get them into the before-school care that is subsidized which for these very low-income parents means it would be practically free!"

"Where do the kids go who are dropped off that early?" I asked.

"On the playground, or they sit in the hallways. You know, at least they're in a safe space if they're sitting in the hallways. On my way to work in the morning, I see three Hispanic mothers who gather at the corner, and you know what they do? They walk their middle schoolers over to the middle school so they can make sure there is no trouble on the way to school. And they wait with them until the bell rings and the kids can go inside. That's what a good parent does!"

I assumed Ms. Hurley would consider me a "good" parent even though I did not walk my middle schooler to school. If so, what was the difference between me and the "bad" parents she was telling me about?

Ms. Hurley continued, "Or when the parents won't even buy their kid boots. That's what happened last year, our principal told a parent that her child needed boots, and she said 'well, you buy them, then!' Yeah, I would like to have time to meet their demands, but I don't even have time to do planning with my co-teacher! I use a bathroom that I have to wipe away urine and feces before I can even sit down!"

Ms. Hurley also told me about the tensions between the teacher's union and the superintendent given that the lesson plan dictate was taking away from instructional time. I asked if the principal at Mason was supportive, and Ms. Hurley told me he was, but that he often "didn't get it" either, thinking she had far more time than she did to accomplish what she needed to accomplish. He was in his mid-thirties she told me and had made mistakes (which she did not seem to want to elaborate on) but he was trying to correct them. Ms. Hurley believed he meant well, but it also seemed that she wanted to see him do some things differently. He was not someone who apologized directly, she told me, but instead would offer verbal praise as a way to make amends.

I asked Ms. Hurley if she thought Mason was treated differently from other schools in the district.

"I think so," she replied. "Mason was the first all-inclusion school, for example. I am not sure how that was decided. I mean, I think it's a good idea, but why was our school chosen? The superintendent eats breakfast where my husband and I often eat as well. One morning when I saw him, I went over and asked him why we were going to be the first all-inclusion school. He didn't have a good answer and we talked about the weather for a minute, and that was it. Friendly, you know. And he would never say this to me, he's friendly to me, but then I heard he went to a meeting with the teachers' union and said 'Linda Hurley interrupted my breakfast and wanted to know why Mason was going to be the only all-inclusion school.' And he said it kind of jokingly, but you know, why shouldn't I ask him? It's something that directly affects me and how often do I get a chance to talk to him?"

This vignette illustrates patently the lack of power, authority, and autonomy teachers often feel as they try to navigate the organizational complexes of District 21. A fundamental complaint that Ms. Hurley voices, as did several teachers in this study, is that no one in a position of authority in District 21 has realistic expectations of what teachers should be accomplishing given the limited amount of time they have and the scope of problems students bring with them to school, particularly at Mason and Helis. Yet, when problems arose, teachers would often lay blame with students' parents, especially if they were minority parents since it was the minority students who generally struggled in their classes.

Blaming parents for underperforming students was not the only consequence, however, of the organizational complexes in District 21 and the system of education in the U.S. Other outcomes that were particularly problematic include devaluing the importance of teachers' work, the surveillance of teachers, and holding teachers responsible for meeting myriad demands without providing them with the requisite resources for success. In the following, I offer a discussion of each of these issues as examples of the organizational complexes in which teachers participate on a daily basis, organizational complexes that provide a context for understanding how teachers think about and how they do race and gender in the classroom. In particular, the two foci I believe are most salient for informing our understanding of these attitudes and behaviors are policy and privilege. In the next chapter, I explore the countervailing forces of privilege that mitigate teachers' potential for serving as social justice advocates, but in this chapter I identify some of the ways teachers' authority and autonomy are inhibited by policies mandated by the superintendent and school board in District 21.

FIVE MINUTES IN THE GRAND SCHEME OF THINGS

A common complaint teachers often talked about in our discussions was the lack of respect with which they thought teachers were treated in District 21 and in society in general. Mr. Hamilton elucidates this frustration with an example of a recent dispute between the superintendent, District 21 teachers, and the local teachers' union:

> Mr. Hamilton: I don't think teachers have figured out if they're blue collar or white collar yet. For example, I belong to a teachers' union that I really believe has overplayed its hand in many respects. Um, I believe that oftentimes our national union asks for things that are not good for students. Like we fight tooth and nail against a longer school day, even though that is exactly what students need. They need a longer school day and extended year. But at the same time, we have an administration that is extremely disrespectful of us at every turn, and is not willing to give teachers their due, and hasn't really decided how much is it worth having fantastic people to teach kids how to read, how to write, how to do math—

> LCS: Are you speaking of District 21?

> Mr. Hamilton: I think in this district in particular and also in general. I think that teachers' unions have been a scapegoat in the reform movement for quite some time but then you have to fight tooth and nail for everything you can get in terms of your working conditions. You know, right now we just had a grievance cited against us, our teachers' union. Our bell rings at 9:00. Our day's supposed to start at 9:05. And it's hard to communicate to parents, for example, that if I'm with students, I'm teaching. The moment that bell rings I am working, you know. When I sign my kids up for a half-hour piano lesson, I don't get thirty-five minutes, you know. So that extra five minutes is five minutes that I'm not making my copies, that I'm not returning my phone calls. And if it's five minutes that I am not getting paid for, then it's five minutes, and it's hard because you don't want to—I'm trying to explain what the challenge of teaching is—that there's a real lack of prestige. There's a real lack I think on the part of teachers of not understanding are we blue collar or are we white collar? In the sense of blue collar, it means we toe the union line. We grab for that five minutes for whatever it gets, you know. Whereas white collar is like we'll figure this out in a way that's good for kids but then you can expect to pay a professional salary. We want to be treated like professionals. I think that's been a big challenge. Um, seeing myself as a professional, but at the same point living in a world that does not see me that way, so...

> LCS: And do you mean that about Lakeview in particular, or just in general?

> Mr. Hamilton: Definitely general, but there's definitely some real things in Lakeview that I've noticed. That and, for example, this five minutes idea. Our superintendent, for example, will say things like "so the five minutes you

spend walking your kids to class is not instructional time and it's time we don't have to pay you for it dah dah dah dah dah. It doesn't violate your contract this, this, this, this." And our superintendent will say things like that. It's like well then you don't understand what my job is then because if I am with students, I am teaching. That is what I am doing, and it's not about the five minutes as such because its five minutes—you know, what's five minutes in the grand scheme of things? It's about the sense of we agreed to this, and yet this is now coming.

In this exchange, Mr. Hamilton reveals a number of important challenges that teachers face as they try to navigate the ruling relations in District 21. As Mr. Hamilton points out, there are several positions adopted by the National Education Association (NEA) that he does not support. Yet, Mr. Hamilton acknowledges the need for teachers' unions in light of the lack of prestige attached to teaching and the lack of understanding on the part of parents, administrators and the local school board, as to what their everyday lives in the classroom entail. Further, the question Mr. Hamilton raises as to whether teaching is essentially white collar work or blue collar work is also relevant to the observation of teachers. While teaching is generally considered a highly trained profession that carries with it a great deal of autonomy, the organizational complexes in District 21 are increasingly moving towards more surveillance of teachers.

THE LESSON PLAN DICTATE AND THE SURVEILLANCE OF TEACHERS

Teachers at Morgan, Mason, and Helis know that at any time during the school day their principal can come into their classroom to observe their behavior. In fact, a major justification for the recent lesson plan dictate is that the principal or superintendent should be able to look at a teacher's lesson plan and know what to expect if they were to walk into a teacher's classroom on any given day at any given time. Of course, anyone who spends even a small amount of time in an elementary school classroom would realize the absurdity of this expectation; indeed, the assumption being that the school day will run perfectly as scheduled, allowing teachers to stick expediently to their lesson plans:

Ms. Norman: Their [superintendent and school board] idea that if we walk into your room on such and such a day we will know what you are going to be teaching because this is your lesson plan—well, the truth is, I can do a whole week and by Wednesday I'm rebooting and changing and adjusting which is *teaching*. Everybody does that, so this whole idea that you're scripting out your lessons—I, it just doesn't make sense, you know. And I don't think you can possibly have, I mean, my cohort in here is so different than the other fifth grade teacher's cohort. There is no possible way we could be, even if we're teaching the same reading lesson, it's not looking the same. I mean, the differentiation isn't even the same, you know. I mean, you might have a couple of outcomes that you want, you know, you want to have, on understanding certain vocabulary or some sort of like synthesis of information or whatever, but the first and second grade readers in my class, their [work] is going to look a whole lot different than, you know, and it's going to be taught to them in a whole different way. I'm not writing all that out! (laughs) It's like, no way!

LCS: It sounds like the superintendent and school board need to come spend time in your classroom.

Mr. Norman: They do! They really do! No, they honestly—they really do!

Further, while it may seem obvious that working with a classroom full of children is more likely than not to bring unexpected challenges that can derail a lesson plan, teachers knew there could be penalties if a person in a position of authority came in to observe their classroom and they were not where they were supposed to be in their lesson plans. Ms. Hurley illustrates this point in the following conversation we had one morning in her classroom while her students were at the library:

LCS: You mentioned he [the principal] may be coming in today? Does he come in to visit or to check what you are doing often?

Ms. Hurley: He does formal observations, but today is a day we were supposed to give him this lesson plan, like twice a month we're supposed to give him one, and he goes to the superintendent's meeting and the superintendent says, 'I want to see an example of an excellent lesson plan for third grade in a gen ed classroom,' and he's got to look in his notebook and pull one out. So every teacher who teaches reading had to turn in a lesson plan today. It wasn't so long, but it took two hours to do, two hours that I should have been getting ready to teach, I should have been looking for the highlighters, I should have been looking for the worksheet, and rereading the teacher's guide because I know what I am doing. But, um, he got his lesson plan and the plan is he is supposed to just pick one and observe and see if the lesson plan is being followed. So, in other words, if I'm teaching math when I am supposed to be teaching reading he's going to have an issue. So I've got to stick to the schedule because it's all about marching in unison these days. There's very little room for a teachable moment.

In these exchanges, both Ms. Norman and Ms. Hurley express their frustration with the new policy concerning written lesson plans adopted by the superintendent and school board members, individuals who rarely visit their classrooms, let alone spend a substantive amount of time with them and their students in order to fully grasp the challenges they face on a daily basis.

Teachers expressed frustration with other forms of surveillance that took place within their schools as well. For example, this year Morgan welcomed a new principal when its former principal, who was much beloved by the teachers and staff, decided to retire. On a couple of occasions when I was doing my classroom observations I noticed the new principal, Mr. Brixton, would come into a classroom unannounced, sit down, observe the teacher while typing feverishly on his laptop, and then leave. I asked Ms. Parker once what he was doing when he came into the classrooms and she told me that she was not sure. I also asked Ms. Lopez about this since she is the union representative at Morgan. She told me that she did not know either, but that she had received complaints from teachers who were upset that Mr. Brixton had not disclosed what he was doing when he came into their classrooms recording information on his laptop. The secrecy surrounding Mr. Brixton's visits and the climate of suspicion it created did not bode well with a number of teachers including Ms. Lopez who stated she had been hoping for more collaboration from him as a new principal but that he was probably acting on orders he was receiving from the "higher-ups." After Mr. Brixton was made aware that some of the teachers were upset by this practice, he disclosed at a staff meeting that when he came into the classrooms he was evaluating the teachers based on approximately thirty different assessment points. This will apparently culminate in a body of data he will be collecting over the school year. At the time I conducted my research, no teacher seemed to know how the body of data would essentially be used.

Interestingly, according to Ms. Lopez, teachers generally come to her when they have these types of complaints since she is the union representative but when she raises their concerns in staff meetings, she told me, teachers who forged the original complaint will oftentimes not speak up. From Ms. Lopez's perspective, she essentially ends up being "the one holding the bag." Indeed, Ms. Lopez is considering resigning as the school union representative because of all the extra time it requires. Extra time is a precious commodity for the teachers in this study, and it is oftentimes further devalued when new educational initiatives are handed down. Inclusion offers an important case in point.

CONFRONTING UNREALISTIC DEMANDS: THE CASE OF INCLUSION

If there was one challenge every teacher in this study could agree on it was that there were not enough hours in the day to accomplish all that the superintendent, school board, and their principals expected of them. This was immediately obvious to me once I began my classroom observations. I would often marvel at how District 21 could expect their teachers to meet the numerous demands they placed upon them since teachers were often not provided with the requisite resources necessary to implement district policies as effectively as possible. This was nowhere more obvious than in the case of inclusion. As Ms. Stevens told me, "People love the idea of inclusion. People love the idea of kids being included in the classroom." However, as Ms. Stevens also made clear there is a breakdown between supporting the idea of inclusion and implementing it effectively in the classroom. The following field notes detail my experience in one inclusion classroom in District 21.

> Field Notes: February 14, 2011, Kindergarten Inclusion Class, Mason Elementary
>
> Mr. Williams has a number of students who need special attention in his classroom. First, there is Tia. Developmentally she seems to be on the level of a 3 or 4 year old. She finds it hard to sit still and follow directions. She constantly agitates her classmates. She leaves the classroom without permission. Then, there's RJ. He has a speech impediment and like Tia finds it very difficult to sit still and follow instructions. He is constantly up and into things. I have not witnessed him be violent but Mr. Williams tells me that he does act out against him and his classmates. Then, there's Billy, who has a very violent temperament. He damages classroom materials and threatens adults and children. Mr. Williams mentioned that parents from other classrooms have complained because he was harassing their children on the playground. And there are also several other children in this class who struggle to stay on task.
>
> Mr. Williams' class is chaotic much of the time. The small handful of children who are what teachers might call "school ready" receive little attention to progress further because Mr. Williams' time has to be taken up with so many of the other children who need extra support. He oftentimes has to remove a child from his class for being disruptive and take them to the office. This does not seem to do much good as once the child returns they begin to engage in the same behaviors. Mr. Williams has a special education aid that comes in for a little while during the day but she seems just as frustrated by the distractions in the class as Mr. Williams. He tells me repeatedly how happy he is to have me in the classroom as he "could certainly use more help."

While Mr. Williams' classroom was not typical of all the inclusion classrooms I observed, I did have a number of inclusion teachers besides Mr. Williams share stories of similar challenges they had either personally experienced or heard of from other teachers. Ms. Hurley was one such teacher. When I asked Ms. Hurley about her experiences with inclusion, she did not mince words:

> Yeah, it's another good idea that's run off the track. See, here's the problem with new ideas in education and particularly District 21, is that new ideas are very, very cool, you know. And usually when the superintendent there's this new idea, this new initiative, we want to incorporate it, generally there's a seed of something that really needs to be tended very carefully. We don't tend it.

We just kind of throw it out there in the soil and if it takes, it takes, and if it doesn't, whatever grows grows. And if it's some kind of a monster plant, it's a monster plant. And we're growing a monster plant right now. Because you cannot have inclusion of every single child. That's the first thing that they don't realize at the administration building. I'm a teacher. I'm not a speech pathologist. I am not a, a physical therapist, an occupational therapist. As long as we have, special ed teachers running back and forth, putting out fires, and, you know, teachers who are not assigned to one classroom all day as a teaching partner, and given enough time to plan to really differentiate for these children and for all children if they need it, it's a half-assed plan.

Inclusion in District 21 is currently being rolled out by grade level. General education teachers in grades kindergarten through third grade are supposed to have special education co-teachers who spend half of their time in one inclusion classroom and the other half of their time in another inclusion classroom. Indeed, the very concept of an "inclusion" class is reminiscent of traditional tracking in that an inclusion class theoretically contains all the students in a particular grade with IEPs. However, this is usually not the case in practice as some students in non-inclusion classrooms are tested and granted IEPs in the course of a school year and are not moved from their classroom to an "inclusion class." After observing inclusion classes and talking with inclusion teachers and co-teachers, I found numerous examples of negligible resources needed to implement inclusion as intended, in addition to other emergent problems that were not being addressed.

First, there were teachers' concerns about whether or not inclusion teachers were receiving the human resources needed in order to effectively implement inclusion. Mr. Swain served on the committee that was successful in bringing inclusion to District 21. However, he was not happy with how the policy was ultimately ushered in:

Mr. Swain: I think something happened, um, as the planning was taking place, that some of the things were sort of rushed through. I think, um, I'm not sure if the infrastructure is really in place to do it in a way that would benefit teachers and students. So I'm not really happy with what I see as far as, um, how it's been implemented so far. I think that ultimately it should benefit students, but I also think that you have to have enough, um, support in place in order to make it truly effective depending on the types of students you have included in the classrooms.

LCS: This is recurring theme I am finding among inclusion teachers: where are the resources?

Mr. Swain: I think that's true. I think, but I think that's something unless you actually see a classroom in action often you can sort of overlook, and I think that's what politicians do. I don't think they really truly realize what teachers are confronted with.

This exchange with Mr. Swain illustrates that while teachers may serve on committees to explore new educational initiatives, it is no guarantee they will be able ensure that teachers' needs in the classroom are met. Further, these types of committees typically only submit recommendations to the superintendent and school board with regard to educational policy; the provisions that are ultimately adopted may not reflect all or even most of the committee's recommendations. For example, although several teachers served on the exploratory committee instrumental in bringing inclusion to District 21, as Mr. Swain points out, in the end the resources to meet the committee's recommendations were not provided or certain concerns the committee raised were not accounted for, such as providing inclusion classrooms with a full-time special education co-teacher.

Not only did teachers at Morgan, Mason, and Helis have concerns about the lack of extra staff to implement inclusion successfully, but about the competence of the resource help that was available. This was a challenge Mr. Williams was facing in his classroom described in the previous vignette. As the teacher of the kindergarten inclusion class, he had been assigned a part-time special education co-teacher at the beginning of the year. However, shortly after the school year started his co-teacher took a leave of absence to attend to family problems. Mr. Williams was then assigned a number of substitute co-teachers who oftentimes had no previous teaching experience:

> Mr. Williams: So I've had a substitute and a different sub and a different sub and a different adult and a different adult every day. And I also have one of the most challenging classrooms that I've ever had in eighteen years. I would say *the* most challenging class.

> LCS: You said this was probably the most challenging class you have had in all these years, are there other things I need to be aware of before I observe your classroom?

> Mr. Williams: No, because you can watch and just see how I do it because all these people here, no social worker, no psychologists have really sat in there with a pencil and said nothing and tried to write it down and this is eighty-seven days today. Eighty-seven days I've been working on it and…so it would be cool to see what you could, what you get out of it. Because basically you know I've got a really violent situation which has gotten, which I've been able to change, incur by myself basically because I've had new substitutes, first-year subs, people who were truck drivers last year, they come in, and they could be anybody, so they're not necessarily trained in this.

Once again in this dialogue, a teacher expresses frustration that the difficulties they encounter in the classroom largely go unobserved by persons they believe are in a position to help. In fact, I was initially shocked to learn that the administration at Mason would allow for such high turnover among the teaching staff in a classroom like Mr. Williams, one that had a number of severe, demonstrable challenges, not to mention hiring or appointing teaching staff that had no former training as teachers. However, since teachers' aid positions pay minimum wage and require only a high school diploma, the staffing challenges Mr. Williams faces make sense.

In the end, instead of placing a full-time special education co-teacher in each inclusion classroom, the district decided to split special education co-teachers between inclusion classrooms. When the special education (inclusion) co-teacher is working in one of their assigned classrooms, a teachers' aid typically replaces them in their other assigned classroom. Therefore, for some portion of the day the students tend to have access to a certified special education co-teacher in the classroom and the other portion of the day is typically spent with a teachers' aid. Principals do tend to give hiring preference to teachers' aid applicants who are certified, but, again, because these positions only pay minimum wage, certified teachers who take these positions often see them (hopefully) as steppingstones to getting their own classrooms.

A second concern teachers expressed with regard to inclusion is that in order for inclusion to be effectively implemented teachers, co-teachers, and other specialists must have time available to effectively plan curricula in order to meet the needs of inclusion students. This was rarely the case in practice. Indeed, it was the most commonly cited concern of teachers who worked with inclusion students, including Ms. Norman, the fifth grade inclusion teacher at Helis:

> We have—the other inclusion teacher—absolutely no common time at all! Even morning and afternoon because, you know, they've got, we've all got meetings before and after school, too. So it's been really, really difficult in that regard. I mean, it's not, it's the social worker and the speech pathologist and all of that, it's impossible to find a time to say this is when we're going to be working, you know, how this is going to look for you when we're doing [the curriculum], you know. We don't do that. We don't have that ability.

Further, there were a number of unintended consequences of this lack of planning time. For example, while in theory classroom teachers and special education co-teachers are supposed to equally share the responsibilities of the classroom, because teachers and co-teachers rarely have time to plan, it is often the classroom teacher who assumes the authority for structuring the class. This, of course, often relegates co-teachers, highly trained certified teachers in their own right, to the role of teachers' aids.

Finally, a number of teachers with whom I worked were also concerned about the "blanket" nature of District 21's inclusion policy. Indeed, any student with an IEP was to be integrated into a general education classroom regardless of the nature of their disability. An "inclusion class" may therefore include one student with a speech impediment while another "inclusion class" may contain five children with several emotional and behavioral disorders. Given the open-ended nature of this policy, several teachers expressed concerns as to whether it was adequately meeting the needs of the students who it intended to serve, including Ms. Lopez, who felt that rather than throw every IEP child into an inclusion classroom each individual child's needs should be evaluated.

> What is best for the child? What is the least restrictive environment? Are we really doing—we have to look at each individual child and really look to see if we're doing them a, a service or a disservice to putting them into a regular classroom. I mean, there's so many factors. How much of the time in a regular classroom if any, or you know, or how little time out of a regular classroom? So are we really doing that? Are we really looking at the individual child? I don't think so. I think we're making, *they're* [superintendent and school board] making big decisions, you know, sweeping decisions.

In addition, there were related concerns about how to protect and meet the needs of teachers and non-IEP students in inclusion classrooms when problems arose particularly with regard to violence, something Ms. Jackson had firsthand experience of as a teacher in an inclusion classroom:

> And like last year I had a student who is now in a behavioral [program] and he walked in the door and he would have these episodes that were dangerous. And he, at some point, um, actually came after me and like tried to hit me—I mean, he's in first grade but he was big and strong and he would have to be restrained, physically on many occasions and he had to be hospitalized a couple of times. Um, and it was so stressful for me that I was like having Posttraumatic [Stress Syndrome]. I was just really trying to keep the rest of the kids safe.

I also witnessed episodes of violence from a white boy in Mr. Williams' kindergarten inclusion class. Indeed, once while working in this classroom I placed a picture the boy had drawn out of his reach after it had first been confiscated by Mr. Williams and the student went and took it from Mr. Williams' desk. The little boy clenched his fists and demanded I give him his picture back or he would kick me. I also watched this boy threaten violence against his classmates and destroy classroom property. As previously mentioned, Mr. Williams also had two other students in his class who would frequently leave the room and have to be brought back, ignore his instructions, and mistreat their classmates and classroom materials.

In the end, the challenges of inclusion that several of the teachers I worked with referenced—lack of teaching support in the classrooms, lack of time for teachers to adequately plan curricula and activities with co-teachers, lack of special education training among teachers and teachers' aids, lack of support in general—actually reflect once again the alienation and powerlessness teachers often feel when new educational initiatives are handed down. Indeed, when it comes to these new policies, teachers are generally expected to *make it work* with little or no authority in the matter. Further, when educational policies like inclusion are revisited in school board meetings, often those teachers asked to speak to the board on behalf of the policy are those who support the policy and can report some degree of success. When this happens, it once again serves to legitimate the ruling relations and organizational complexes in which the teachers participate.

CONCLUSION: TEACHERS' PERSPECTIVES ON RACE AND GENDER IN THE CONTEXT OF RULING RELATIONS

During the year I conducted this research, a public discussion took place between the superintendent and school board about whether tens of thousands of dollars should be spent on bringing in an educational consulting firm from California to study equity issues in District 21. I found this both amusing and tragic. Surely, if the superintendent and school board had simply contacted their own institutional research office they would have found that I and perhaps others who were also well acquainted with the schools had already conducted such research, and at least in my case, were willing to confer free of charge. I reached out to a local school board member, Ann, whom a couple of parents in the district had recommended, assuring me she would be both interested and sensitive towards the issues I studied.

Ann and I met at a local coffee shop one afternoon soon after I finished data collection. I shared with her some of my concerns, particularly with regards to differentiation and inclusion. When I finished telling her about the challenges I observed in the classrooms, she thought on this for a moment and then asked, "Would you be willing to conduct some diversity training with the teachers on these issues?" My heart sank. While I told Ann I was willing to help pro bono in whatever way I could, I made it clear that I did *not* think the teachers were the source of the trouble nor would *diversity training* resolve what were essentially structural problems. Ann nodded her head, told me that she would take the information I had shared back to the school board, and she would be in touch. I never heard from her again.

The challenges of inclusion, the five minute grievance cited against the teachers' union, and the lesson plan dictate, all reveal a common problem that continually emerged in my discussions with teachers at Morgan, Mason, and Helis: a disconnect exists between those who mandate educational policy, specifically the superintendent and the school board, and the teachers who are expected to implement these policies. As illustrated in this chapter, a number of the teachers with whom I worked felt alienated from the policy-

making process even though teachers commonly served on committees exploring new educational initiatives. It is perhaps no surprise, therefore, that
teachers in this study generally welcomed the opportunity to express their
frustrations to a researcher who wanted to know what *they* thought about
District 21's policies, someone who saw value in their perspectives as *insid-
ers* who were living with District 21 policies everyday in the classroom.

In the end, the map of ruling relations (Figure 4.1) provides an important
analytical tool for understanding teachers' attitudes about race and gender
and their behaviors towards race- and gender-related issues. For example, the
system of organizational complexes that teachers participate in rewards them
for following the rules, not rocking the boat. As Angela Valenzuela points
out, education is a bureaucratically inefficient system that offers no incentives for prioritizing students' welfare over following "the rules." (1999:
256) Further, the number of demands put upon teachers ensures there is little
time left in their day to address concerns beyond teaching students basic
curriculum and trying to manage the classroom environment. Therefore, to a
large extent the organizational complexes in which the teachers participate
actively subvert their potential to address institutional racism and sexism
whether they acknowledge they exist or not.

While all three policy examples illustrated in this chapter clearly point to
the decreasing power, authority, and autonomy teachers have over their own
work, it is important to remember that teachers are not just at the mercy of
the institution; they are at the same time agents of the institution. For example, there are areas over which teachers clearly can and do assert their authority. This is particularly the case when it comes to their relationships with
their students and with parents. It is in this context teachers' attitudes towards
race and gender and the institutional structure in which they participate intersect. Further, it is also where the countervailing effects of individual, student,
and community-based privileges emerge that, like the structure of contemporary schooling, mitigate teachers' efforts to address institutional racism and
sexism. Each type of privilege is discussed in detail in the next chapter.

Chapter Five

The Countervailing Forces of Privilege

In the previous chapter, I mapped the ruling relations the teachers in this study participate in on a regular basis. In particular, I highlighted three recent policy initiatives mandated by the superintendent and school board that usurp teachers' authority, power, and autonomy. Given the organizational complexes teachers must continually navigate, it seems reasonable to ask whether we can expect them to serve as social justice advocates when there are so many pressing concerns they must attend to including (1) differentiating their curriculum to meet as many of the individual needs of their students as possible; (2) working with RTI students for a mandated number of minutes every day; (3) integrating IEP students as fully as possible into the regular classroom; (4) maintaining communication with parents, teachers, and other resource staff; (5) attending mandatory faculty meetings and in-service training; (6) writing out lesson plans, grading assignments, and developing classroom activities; (7) preparing students to take the high-stakes test that might impact their retention; (8) and myriad other responsibilities so easily overlooked unless you regularly spend time in an elementary school classroom. Of course, this question assumes that teachers are indeed aware of institutional racism and sexism to begin with, and desire to address both—a position not taken by most of the teachers in this study. The point is that even for the teachers who do want to serve as social justice advocates in the classroom, the organizational complexes in which they work continually undermine their ability to do so. This is to say nothing of the other countervailing forces at work, in particular, the pervasiveness of privilege.

In general, I found three types of privilege that work against teachers addressing contemporary, institutional racism and sexism: privilege associated with individual teachers' social locations, privilege associated with white students and their families, and privilege associated with the community of

Lakeview. It is important to note that each type of privilege while interrelated is also distinct; indeed, privilege can take both the form of conferred dominance in which one group is given power over another group, and the form of unearned entitlements in which one group is given access to resources or things of value that are systematically denied to other groups (McIntosh 1992). Individual privilege among teachers, for example, primarily takes the form of conferred dominance while student privilege and community privilege often manifest as unearned entitlements. In this chapter, I discuss all three types of privilege and provide examples of what each looks like in the color- and gender-blind classroom.

TEACHERS' PRIVILEGE

One underlying factor in teachers' resistance to acknowledging *and* addressing institutional racism and sexism is their own privilege. At times this privilege may be a result of their whiteness, their masculinity, their social class, and/or their heterosexuality. The intersection of these as well as many other identities creates a unique social location for each teacher in this study; the privilege shared by all the teachers, however, is that associated with their advanced teacher training and socialization into the education system in the U.S. Teachers are essentially highly trained "experts" who are granted authority as agents of the educational system to promote and sanction what they believe is the proper family-school relationship (Lareau 1987). The privilege afforded to teachers as a result of occupying this role is particularly evident in their definitions of what constitutes "good" parents and "bad" parents, and their construction and enforcement of a dominant classroom culture.

GOOD PARENT, BAD PARENT

When I asked teachers about common obstacles their students faced, inevitably the discussion turned to their students' family lives. Indeed, teachers' first line of defense when questioned about their responsibility in the numerous problems associated with contemporary schooling was generally, 'well, there is only so much we can do in the classroom,' some version of which I heard on several occasions in the course of my research. While teachers told me they derived great personal satisfaction from watching their students' progress academically, socially, and emotionally, they generally cited the amount and the quality of *parental support* students had access to as the single strongest predictor of student success. The common wisdom was that despite the efforts of the best teachers any potential academic progress was undermined by "poor parenting." In my conversations with Ms. Hurley, she shared a number of stories about the problems her students had to cope with:

> I, you know, I had a little boy who was homeless. Came in one day without his homework and I said, "Why didn't you do your homework?" He said, "I tried to do it but there wasn't enough light in the back of a car when we were driving around looking for a bed. My grandmother finally let us in but it was three o'clock." So I said, "You know what, you do it now. That's not a good enough excuse for me because you owe it to yourself to get your homework done. Because you have to make better choices than your mother was able to make." Because he could identify the difficult choices—she had children really young, she wasn't married, she didn't get a good education. He knew all of that, so he did his homework. I wanted to cry and hug him, but I didn't, you know.

Interestingly, in our conversations Ms. Hurley would make reference to several macro-level factors that underlie the struggles her students face—poverty, teenage parenthood, homelessness—yet her explanation for why these students were in crisis was always rooted in an individual-level understanding. In the anecdote she shares about her student who was unable to do his homework because he and his family were homeless, she uses abstract liberalism (Bonilla-Silva 2006) to point the finger at the bad decisions on the part of the students' mother; in fact, she tells her student that, "he has to make *better* decisions than his mother." Alternately, she might have implicated the current economic recession or racial discrimination in housing, for example.

In the end, individual-level explanations for social problems like homelessness both sustain and reflect the color- and gender-blind classroom. In this learning environment, academic success is reified by teachers as a panacea for bad choices: had Ms. Hurley's student's mother *chosen* to get a "good education" (which she assumes was an option on the table to begin with) instead of *choosing* to have children too young and out-of-wedlock, as Ms. Hurley implies, her student would not have missed his homework assignment because he was looking for a place to sleep. Of course, Ms. Hurley's own privilege is revealed as she passes judgment on what constitutes the appropriate circumstances with which to have children including parental age, education-level, and family configuration.

Similarly, when I spoke with Ms. Chang who teaches at Helis, a Title I school that like Mason has a much higher proportion of transient students since so many families are in crisis, she expressed empathy for the challenges the student population at her school faced, but then again revealed her own privilege by questioning the caliber of parents who would move their children from one school to another in the middle of the school year as if the parents had complete autonomy in the matter:

> There's a bunch of difficult kids in Ms. Norman's room that were not here in third grade. Yeah, so if you show up in fifth grade, imagine what kind of student you're going to get because who moves in fifth grade?!? I mean, who moves in the middle of the year?!? I got a kid in February—who moves?!?

> Nobody else does, you know? Who moves? Basic success is if you're at one
> school from kindergarten through fifth grade, continued schooling, okay?

Note that in the conversations with Ms. Hurley and Ms. Chang not only are students' home lives understood primarily as the result of "bad choices," but both teachers continually infer a link between structural-level problems like poverty and parents who do not *care* for their children in one way or the other. In fact, this was a frequent occurrence in the stories teachers told about the struggles many of their students and their students' families had to contend with: economic disadvantage was almost always linked with an inability for parents to provide love and emotional support to their children. Poor parents were *damaged* parents. For example, Ms. Stevens presented an interesting paradox when she disclosed that it was through her experiences teaching in an all-white school that she knew she wanted to work in a racially diverse environment.

> Ms. Stevens: And I student taught in Cross Creek, at Parker Elementary School, which is like the most homogenous group of children, probably that I've ever seen in a school. They were like all just white, English-speaking, middle- upper class families, just totally not what I wanted to do, and I knew that when I was student teaching. I'd say, "This isn't where I want to be," and—
>
> LCS: How did you know that?
>
> Ms. Stevens: I don't know, I just felt, I was, I've always felt the reason I wanted to be a teacher is because I want to like help those kids that feel—you know, those kids [at Parker Elementary] are going to be fine, whether or not they have me as their teacher, really in the long run. They have parents who love and care about them, and help them with their homework. I wanted to be with kids who had challenges at home and saw school as a safe place where they can just have a routine, have someone who cares, you know.

Again, note the comparisons Ms. Stevens draws between her students at Parker Elementary and those with whom she now teaches at Helis. Students at Parker have parents who love them and care about whether or not they succeed in school; poor, minority children do not because they automatically come from "challenged" homes. On more than one occasion Ms. Stevens indicated she saw herself in a "white savior" role (Vera and Gordon 2003) at Helis.

In sum, these stories about students and their family lives offer important insights into how teachers' own privilege undermines their ability to serve as social justice advocates in the classroom. In these narratives, teachers situate themselves as "experts," agents of the institution; persons who because of their advanced teacher training and position within the ruling relations of

District 21 are granted authority to deem what constitutes proper care and love of children. They determine whose parents should be commended for doing it "right" and whose parents should be condemned for doing it "wrong" (see also Lareau 2003). Time and again, the circumstances that surround those families that teachers believe fail to provide proper support to their children are understood not as the result of macro-level circumstances that parents are unable to control, but rather personal *choices* on the part of mostly minority parents.

Understanding how teachers' social locations influence their attitudes about what differentiates good parents from bad parents is only one part of the story, however; what is particularly important to recognize is how these social locations are inscribed in geography. The bottom line is that while several teachers in this study grew up in working-class neighborhoods, only three teachers currently live in the city of Chicago in neighborhoods with large percentages of poor and working-class families. Therefore, whether or not teachers grew up in communities similar to those inhabited by their minority students, almost every teacher in this study currently lives in communities that are geographically and ideologically removed from those in which the majority of their poor, minority students reside. This may not only make it difficult for teachers to empathize with these students and their families but lead teachers to draw conclusions about the nature and quality of parental support and love minority students receive without firsthand knowledge (e.g., Delpit 2006; Theoharis and Haddix 2011).

For example, in the following discussion of contemporary problems in schooling and the ways in which they relate to racial inequality, Mr. Gira makes a number of assumptions about minority parents including their inability to form stable family structures. Of course, these assumptions again situate Mr. Gira as the expert on what constitutes *stable family structures*. For instance, Mr. Gira lists a number of responsibilities that "good" parents should fulfill, or in the case of reading, "good" *mothers* should fulfill. The most significant implication of his argument, however, is that "good" parenting and "bad" parenting are a matter of culture (e.g., Bonilla-Silva 2006).

Well, we need more money somewhere; it's got to come from somewhere. Um, and, you know, anyway the government can reconfigure where money is being raised, you know, where it's being utilized and redirect to some of those areas so that, uh, um, they [Black children] have a chance to be successful. I mean, it becomes a money thing as well as it takes time. It's, it's not going to happen overnight and as long as you don't have that family unit at home that's supporting these [Black] kids, and making sure that they get a good breakfast in the morning and that they're really concerned that they're doing their home-work at night, and that the mom started reading to them when they were two or three at least, you know, that's, that stuff doesn't happen overnight and it's going to take a while, but, um, you know, it's like any other development of cultures, that there is, there are areas of our culture that still need a lot more attention. And I think it's, you know, we, we've made so many gains in the last hundred years; it'll take another fifty to one hundred to get where we need to be probably.

The many contradictions in Mr. Gira's dialogue offer a number of powerful insights into how he views the relationship between race, culture, and schooling. On the one hand, his belief that more public monies are needed to address social inequalities appears to offer support for macro-level solutions, presumably in terms of public policy. Yet, given his latter comments that implicate a deficiency in (Black) "culture" as the explanation and possible solution to racial inequalities, the argument that more monies are needed is at best a paternalistic one: what we need to do is help the "Black culture" to assimilate to the dominant culture (which may take another fifty or one hundred years). Mr. Gira further asserts that Black children do not have stable family structures that ensure they are eating nutritiously before they come to school (whether or not parents can afford it) or parents who make sure they do their homework and read to them at early ages (regardless of whether they are working two or three jobs and may not have time to do so). In the end, Mr. Gira's argument is encapsulated by the assertion that racial inequalities can be addressed with the "development" of Black culture. The logic that underpins what distinguishes "developed" and "developing" cultures and "good" parents and "bad parents" appears synonymous.

Interestingly, "good parents" could also present problems for the teachers in this study particularly if they attempted to usurp teachers' authority. This was not unusual in a community like Lakeview with a higher than average number of residents with formal educations. For example, "good" parents could assume the role of "bad" parents, albeit temporarily, if their parenting prevented their children from being able to effectively internalize and observe the classroom culture; in other words, if parents tried to pull rank on the teacher asserting *they,* not the teacher, knew best. In the end, however, it was the teachers who had the authority and power to determine the nature of the classroom culture in which their children interacted everyday, and perhaps not surprisingly it was one that legitimated teachers' positions within the ruling relations.

THE CLASSROOM CULTURE

LCS: Now, with all the challenges that come with teaching, what would you say is the biggest challenge?

Mr. Foy: Well, certainly kids with serious behavioral issues. I'd have to say that's the biggest thing. Kids who, um, for whatever reason are not sure how—

they don't really understand the classroom culture and what it's supposed to be. They don't understand it. Or they're not interested in it, or their interests lay elsewhere. Or there's a lot of stress at home that comes into the class. But it's the kids who, you know, obviously disrupt and make life hard for me and for other students.

Teachers' opinions about whether the parents of their students were "good" or "bad" was also related to how well or how poorly parents' socialization of their children matched the classroom culture (e.g., Lareau 1987; 2003). Teachers provided several insights into the type of culture they tried to cultivate as they talked about what their students needed in order to be successful in their classes. There were, of course, a number of overlapping themes among the teachers in this study, but there were some interesting differences across schools. At Morgan, teachers emphasized the importance of their students being independent and taking risks, good organizational skills and the ability to stay on task, as well as a desire to learn. Teachers at Helis and Mason also mentioned the importance of many of these traits, however, they were more likely than the teachers at Morgan to stress the importance of students being honest, following routines, taking responsibility for their own behavior, learning self-control, and being kind (e.g., Kozol 1991).

According to Annette Lareau (1987), "the social profitability of middle-class arrangements is tied to the schools' definition of the proper family-school relationship." Mr. Hamilton like several teachers in this study, for example, told me the students who struggled in his classes oftentimes could not reconcile the differences between "school culture" and "home culture." According to Mr. Hamilton, "There's just different cultures in school and in home life and not really knowing the expectations then coming here and trying to apply rules from one universe to another universe doesn't always work." Interestingly in my conversation with Mr. Hamilton and in fact all the teachers, no one questioned the legitimacy of the "classroom culture." The concern was whether parents were successfully doing their job to properly socialize their children to accept and value the classroom culture and the culture of contemporary schooling in general.

Further, while each school I worked in established a set of rules to govern students' day, each teacher also had specific rules they expected their students to follow, culminating in a *dominant classroom culture*. While in my observations a few teachers went so far as to refer to their students as "friends," teachers were clearly situated within the dominant classroom culture as the "boss." For example, in the following vignette, Mr. Hamilton is determined to assert his authority by enforcing *the rules*.

Field Notes: Mr. Hamilton's Third Grade General Education Class, October 11, 2010

Mr. Hamilton asks the students to clean their tables. They do so quickly and then come back to the rug for read-aloud. Mr. Hamilton begins by telling the children that he has been very surprised by their behavior this morning, and that he has not been able to give out a lot of rewards for following the rules. He threatens Vikram, who struggles regularly to stay on task and follow instructions, that if his behavior does not improve he will have to stick with an adult the rest of the day and "have no fun." Mr. Hamilton goes back over the rules for read-aloud.

Mr. Hamilton places a book under the document camera and tells the kids to sit with their legs crossed, hands in their lap, with their eyes on the Promethean board. He tells Marcus, Thomas, and Vikram, who do not comply, they are going to have to stay in for recess so that he can go back over the rules with them.

"I think that's fair," Mr. Hamilton tells the three of them. "Does that mean I think you're bad rotten kids?"

"No!" Marcus says. "You think every kid is a good kid."

"That's right," Mr. Hamilton says. He then says to the other children, "Thank you, class, for being patient even though you have lost five minutes of read-aloud time." He attempts to start the story several more times but continues to stop to give behavioral reprimands to Vikram and Thomas.

All of the kids are growing very frustrated, and I am as well. I wonder if it's really necessary that the kids must sit with their legs crossed and hands in their laps. Mr. Hamilton begins again, reads two words, and then informs the kids that the time is up and it is time to line up for lunch. The kids who have been doing what he asked are demonstrably frustrated, and I do not blame them.

As this example illustrates, the classroom culture is built on deference to teachers and to the institution of education. Students—like teachers—who follow *the rules* are rewarded; those who do not are punished. Parents who socialize their children to observe the classroom culture teach them to respect their teacher and classmates, to listen and follow rules and instructions, and make sure their children arrive at school on time and prepared for the day. Again, whether or not parents did this successfully factored into teachers' perceptions of how well they performed their job. It is in this capacity to sanction parents and students that the pervasiveness of teachers' own privilege is most salient.

STUDENTS' PRIVILEGE

When considering inequality in education, inevitably the focus turns to the relationship between poverty and schooling (e.g., Kozol 1991; Farkas 1996; Lent and Figueira 2002). This is reflected in teacher concerns about ISAT scores, for example, since poverty is an underlying variable among the sub-groups that fail to meet standards. Indeed, I recorded numerous examples of the tangible effects of poverty I witnessed in my classroom observations at all three schools particularly with regard to students' inability to grasp basic skills and concepts. Yet, the reason these examples were generally so stark, was because the poverty of students in District 21 schools is at all times juxtaposed to the overwhelming privilege of students in the same district. Teachers are responsible for bridging the socioeconomic chasm between their students, and most talked candidly about this challenge, even making reference at times to inequalities between the "haves" and the "have-nots" in Lakeview. Yet, unearned privilege was not problematized (McIntosh 1992; Hurtado 1996).

While poverty places many students at an obvious disadvantage in terms of mastering the mandated curricula, students who have access to cultural capital, accentuated by their access to social capital via their parent-advocates (e.g., Bourdieu 1986), are consistently at an advantage. These are the students teachers can count on to make AYP each year. Therefore, even though the majority of these privileged students are white, illuminating a clear racial disparity between subgroups, because they exhibit the traits teachers value and seek to cultivate (Lareau 2003) in their classrooms, to problematize students' unearned privilege is tantamount to problematizing the foundation of teachers' educational philosophy (see also Hurtado 1996). In the following, I explore the influence of cultural and social capital in the color- and gender-blind classroom.

THE INFLUENCE OF CULTURAL CAPITAL

According to Amy Orr (2003), children's learning time can be increased as a result of access to educational resources determined by a family's wealth, examples of which may include books, computers, or tutors (283). Indeed, parents at Morgan, and a few other schools in District 21, can literally *buy* a teacher for their child. In the following Ms. Roberts shares her concerns about an annual fundraiser at Morgan:

> You know, you have to pay forty bucks to go to it. It's a event for only parents, only adults. Which right away, I mean, a lot of people don't leave their kids at home for things like that, and I don't know how much it is. Forty dollars or something per person. Um, and they have an auction where, a silent auction

and there are teachers that you can bid on to spend special time outside of school with. So I've brought it up several times at staff meetings because I feel like there's nothing more biased than that event. I mean, the, you know, the only kids that are going to be able to have special time with you are the white privileged or Black [privileged], I mean we do have of course a few, but the privileged kids...that dynamic is 'my mom bought this time for me.' I don't, it just really, really bothers me. You know, I, I do have in my little circle of support and some people don't participate [in the silent auction]. But it hasn't been stopped. You know, and the PTA felt very attacked, like felt like I was not appreciative of all their work and stuff. You know, I, it just wasn't received well. And you know we have a new principal but I don't know that he's—I haven't even brought it up with him. But the teachers didn't stop. I mean, most, I don't know, most, at least half or more still participate after several years and several times of discussing it at staff meetings. Yeah. I was called a socialist.

As Ms. Roberts points out, there are a number of factors that make this particular school fundraiser perhaps the quintessential example of how privilege can secure certain benefits for (white) students above and beyond their less-privileged peers. After all, in addition to parents having the financial resources with which to outbid other parents so their child can have special (private) time with their teacher, they must also be able to pay the forty dollars required to get into the event and be able to secure childcare. What's more, even though Ms. Roberts and a few other teachers at Morgan raised concerns about the fairness of the fundraiser, they were dismissed. In the end, neither the PTA who organized and sponsored the fundraiser, the principal, nor the majority of Morgan teachers apparently saw the event as problematic.

Another type of educational resource that parents could *buy* for their children was the ability to travel. I observed several examples that access to this form of cultural capital (Bourdieu 1986) had on students in the classroom. For example, Ms. Parker was one of several teachers in this study who found that students who had experienced the world outside of Lakeview were able to draw on those experiences to help them understand curriculum. For those students, on the other hand, who had not ventured outside of Lakeview it was difficult at times to conceptualize things like the differences in landforms. Ms. Parker offers a recent example of how she attempted to compensate for the lack of familiarity some of her students had with canyons:

Ms. Parker: Well, we were talking about landforms in second grade right now, so we're talking about canyons. There's a certain group of the class that have been to the Grand Canyons, who have been to canyons here and there. And I was reading about canyons in Peru and hands were going up—"I've been to Peru!" What?!? Really? (laughs) And then you've got this part of your class that haven't been out of Lakeview. And so bringing that together and trying to make sure that everybody kind of—there are days that I don't know. It's, it's really a challenge especially with something that's so, um, experiential like an understanding of what a canyon is. So we looked at photos, you know, we looked at books, but again, it's not the same—

LCS: This is a challenge I'm hearing other teachers talk about. But I'm just curious—do you find among the kids with this, given this range of experiences, um, is there ever any attempt to make the other children who don't have those experiences feel like they're left out? Or do you not see that?

Ms. Parker: By the other children?

LCS: Yes. Is there this sense of 'oh, I know what canyons are, I've been to the Grand Canyon, what's wrong with you that you haven't?'

Ms. Parker: You know, I think working with young children they don't look at things that way. They're so egocentric still that it is all about I want to share about me, you know, and they don't—I don't even think they even think about it in terms yet of that.

While Ms. Parker believed her second graders were still too self-absorbed to intentionally one-up their classmates, I did witness this occur in other classrooms:

Field Notes: Mr. Foy's Fourth Grade General Education Class, October 26, 2010

The students are instructed to continue working on their stories about a place they have traveled. As I walk around the room, I stumble upon this conversation at a table with a white girl, a white boy, a Black girl, and the one Hispanic boy in the class.

The white boy, talking about flying in an airplane says, "First class is so cool. They usually have a plasma TV so you can watch stuff."

The white girl chimes in, "Yes, it's awesome! I remember one time I got to eat the pilot's ravioli!"

I notice the Hispanic boy has tuned out this conversation, and the Black girl at the table just looks at the two of them with a confused look on her face as if they are speaking in a different language.

Whenever possible in my classroom observations, I read students' work, seeking any connections between what they wrote and their social locations, particularly with regard to race, class, and gender. At the elementary level, students' writing assignments often revolved around their own experiences. A common assignment, for example, asked students to write about a recent trip they took. When Mr. Foy assigned this topic, I read every paper possible looking for variations. One white boy wrote of his trip to Scandinavia the past summer, another white girl wrote about her trip to Cape Cod. I also read white students' stories about going to New York and other distant places. The three Black students in Mr. Foy's class wrote about a trip to Six Flags, a trip to Disneyworld, and an uncle's birthday party. There were a few white children who wrote about more modest experiences such as going to a block party and getting a new cat, but when access to cultural capital was evident in students' writing, the students were almost always white.

Finally, a related form of cultural capital that manifests in access to extra-curricular activities, trips to museums, and other cultural venues, also enhances students' ability to make connections to the curricula, thus putting privileged students at an advantage once again. Ms. Chang talks about the benefits of this type of cultural capital in the following:

> In order to make the book that they're [students] reading make sense, they have to have that experience, or a similar experience, and you can't just get that from watching a movie. Um, which I'm finding a lot of people, that's all their doing. They're just watching movies. They're not going to live theatre. And then, also because of No Child Left Behind…because it's so much pressure for us to get all this teaching done, we don't take field trips. But not just because of that one thing. I think also because it's costly. The gas prices went up, so therefore the bus fees went up. So we don't take a lot of field trips. Well, we used to always go to a live theatre show. Kindergarten used to always go to the pumpkin patch. Now, again, with the turning of the economy a lot of these places have closed down, so you have to go further. But they [District 21] don't do those anymore. Which is really too bad because these [low income] kids don't get the experience from their parents. Well, where are they going to get that experience? Now, um, people who don't work with this population, they're like—which are probably the legislators—"You shouldn't, they shouldn't be going on all these fieldtrips. That's just fun! School shouldn't be fun! It should be learning! You should be reading! You should be writing!'" But they don't understand again, that connection. But they're the ones making the laws. And their kids are fine. Well, of course, their kids are fine. They've been taking them to the museum. These kids haven't been to the museum, you know. It's really sad. It's quite, quite sad.

In this excerpt, Ms. Chang makes the argument that students' experiences *outside* the classroom enhance their understanding of the lessons she tries to teach them *in* the classroom. Not only does Ms. Chang lament the loss of some of the fieldtrips that Helis students used to take in order to provide students with extracurricular experiences their parents might not be able to provide for them, but she acknowledges how privilege on the part of those who make educational policy prevents them from realizing the unintended consequences of gutting these programs. As she suggests, politicians who are able to provide these outside experiences for their own children are not necessarily cognizant of the effects that not having access to these extracurricular activities can have on students who come from under-resourced families (or perhaps they know and do not care).

In sum, the disparities between low-income students and privileged students in District 21 are vast. Many students live in families who do not have access to basic resources, while others live in families who vacation in Europe over the summer months. Privileged students, who are most often white, have access to myriad forms of cultural capital that enhance their ability to succeed in school. Poor students, on the other hand, who are most often students of color, are consistently at a disadvantage when it comes to making personal connections to the mandated curriculum, for example. Teachers expressed concern about the disadvantages of these students who through no fault of their own were born into under-resourced families; teachers did not express concern about the students who through no effort of their own were born into privileged families.

SOCIAL CAPITAL: THE (WHITE) PRIVILEGE OF PARENT-ADVOCATES

Ms. Martin's second grade class at Helis is very racially diverse. After several visits, however, I noticed there were a number of white students who tended to dominate most of the class discussions and who often appointed themselves the leaders of group activities. I asked Ms. Martin if there were strategies she used to ensure that minority students also had equal representation in her room.

> I try to create a rapport with the kids first and foremost and build that relationship and "look, hey, you might think that XYZ is smarter than you, it's not true. It's up to you." They're [white students] more aggressive, they push and they push and they're not letting go. Kelly, she is not letting go until you answer and, and she's taking in everything I say. I, I can depend on her to, to reiterate what I'm saying to her to the class, you know, and they push and I'm saying to the, the African American kids, I'm saying, "you've got to push. You've got to be more, raise your hand." Yeah, you know, so you, you have to be as aggressive. They're [white students] aggressive and I keep going back to where it starts. At home. [White] parents are in here, their parents are in here all the time. If one thing doesn't go right, believe me they're coming, they're checking on this, they're doing it...And they constantly see their, their parents and they see that they're invested, you know.

In essence, parents serve the interests of their children (and themselves) when they perform the role of advocate. Indeed, parent-advocates are an important resource for students, a resource rooted in privilege and racial inequality. As Ms. Roberts told me, "Parents who can advocate for their kids get what their kids need, and parents who can't don't."

For example, at the community meeting I attended with Carol Ann Tomlinson, the overarching message of her talk was that "good" teachers are those who differentiate their classrooms, and by doing so teachers can overcome any barriers their students face in their ability to grow academically, socially, and emotionally. Indeed, Tomlinson shared personal anecdotes of disadvantaged students of color she helped to steer onto a path of success as a public school teacher. As I looked around at the almost-all white audience, many nodded in agreement while others voiced their support under their breath. The parents in attendance appeared visibly moved by stories Tomlinson shared of students of color who came from overwhelming circumstances and turned out to be fine upstanding citizens thanks to the dedication of "good" teachers. Even so, parents' questions at the end of the lecture generally focused on Tomlinson's suggestions for how teachers could best serve *their* children.

At times, the advocacy of privileged parents is revealed through their beliefs about how and what their children should learn as in the following example taken from my field notes:

Field Notes: Mr. Foy's Fourth Grade General Education Class, October 5, 2010

As Mr. Foy goes over the math exercises with the students, I am again reminded of how so much has changed from when I was in school. The students are being taught multiple ways to solve math facts including how to come up with "ballpark answers," a form of estimation before actually working the problem. One white girl, Natalia, raises her hand and declares that her dad is confused by the partial sums method she is being taught and that he doesn't like her to do it that way. Mr. Foy calmly suggests that since methods of teaching math have changed maybe Natalia should teach her father some of these new strategies. "No, I don't think it's that he doesn't know how to do it. He gets it, he just doesn't like it." I later overhear this same student remarking to another student about the differences between protons and neutrons that her dad, who has a Ph.D. in physics, taught her. She tells her classmates that he knows what he's talking about.

At other times, the advocacy of privileged parents includes things they do not want for their children, such as a desire to not have them share headphones with their classmates, something white parents concerned about the "hygiene" of other students complained about in Ms. Stevens' dual language class. Still, at other times, parent-advocates expressed concerns about special treatment their children may not be receiving compared to their classmates.

Mr. Hamilton offered an example of this as he discussed his strategy for addressing behavioral challenges in the classroom:

> Yeah, last year, I had some students who received tickets. And how this worked was that tickets were if you needed to be out of your seat, sure, you get three tickets, and you know, you get out of your seat, rip the ticket up, you're done. This was like an add-on [to the school-wide behavioral modification program], my own thing. I had three kids that just weren't getting it the [school-wide program] way. They needed this, and so what they got is tickets and the tickets allowed them to leave their seat and if they didn't use their tickets to leave their seats for like bathroom, for this, for that, at the end of the day they could use it for some extra free time. This was the idea to teach the lesson if you can manage yourself well, you can delay your gratification, then you can get your free time later. Um, being efficient means having more time to do what you want, and so, uh, I have another [white] parent who called and said this was very unfair. "How come my daughter doesn't get tickets, and how come my daughter doesn't get duh duh duh?" And what I said was, "if you would like me to put your daughter on a behavior plan we can do that but the reality is that these other kids their day is pretty awful. Ninety percent of the time that I'm talking to these kids, it's to correct their behavior. It's to say something that's not so nice, and this is one of the few times in the day they can experience some kind of success. Right now, your daughter experiences success most of the time. She really doesn't need this behavior plan, so we're not going to do that."

As these examples show, not only does privilege bring with it cultural capital in the form of extracurricular accouterments that increase students' chances of academic success, but social capital in the form of parent-advocates who ensure their children get all the educational opportunities they believe they *deserve* and that their children are treated fairly in the classroom (if not better). Parent-advocates may also shield their children from participating in activities if they think it is in their best interest. In the end, white privilege grants parents the ability, legitimacy, and authority to *negotiate* with teachers and administrators. This puts teachers in the position of catering to the desires of white parents over and above the desires of parents of color, creating an environment not amenable to addressing institutional discrimination and privilege. Interestingly, the privilege on the part of the primarily white parent-advocates in District 21 is reflective of the privilege associated with the community of Lakeview itself. Ironically, most of these parents as residents of Lakeview consider themselves tolerant, enlightened, and, essentially, "good liberals." There are obvious limits, however, to their progressivism.

PRIVILEGE IN LAKEVIEW

Despite a commitment to the ideals of social justice, Lakeview is a town that is very racially segregated and where distinctions between the poor, who are mostly Black and Hispanic, and the very privileged are readily apparent. Interestingly, when I used to share that I was a resident of Lakeview with those who were even remotely familiar with the town, one of the first things they generally exclaimed was how wonderfully diverse it was. Indeed, white residents of Lakeview often cite diversity as its number one selling point, especially compared to towns farther north where Lakeviewers would *never* live because it is "too white." Indeed, when I asked Mr. Gold why he thought gender inequality was no longer a problem in schooling, he offered the following commentary about the nature of the community:

> It's a community that kind of, people who choose to live here and teach here, come with a predisposition to kind of viewing people to the best extent they can. It's just that type of community we live in, you know. You don't live in Lakeview if you are a different type of person generally. Now, all the teachers generally live in Lakeview, or they are people who have been associated with Lakeview a long time. And the ones who come from outside soon learn the type of personality and the type of community we live in. And you'd be very out of place if your attitudes were racist, and you know, homophobic, or you had gender preferences.

Yet, as a former resident of Lakeview and as a sociologist who studied teachers and students in District 21, I uncovered numerous examples of contradictions between the ideology of the "good" (white) liberals who inhabit the town and whose children attend public schools, and their beliefs and behaviors concerning inequality. As Ms. Lopez told me, "people say they want diversity, but not in my backyard." Paradoxically, it is Lakeview's reputation for social progressiveness, I believe, that shields many privileged residents from being forced to acknowledge the pervasiveness of racial and gender inequality.

NOT IN MY BACKYARD: THE LIMITS OF LIBERALISM

The teachers with whom I worked frequently shared examples of the degree to which District 21 and people in Lakeview embrace diversity, yet there were obvious limits. I decided to ask the few teachers who spoke particularly passionately about inequality in schooling and engaged in activities in the classroom to further equality, even if only at the individual-level, how much support they felt they would receive if they were to address institutional racism and sexism. The following conversation between Ms. Parker and I one afternoon in her classroom encapsulates the parameters of how far "good liberals" were willing to go (or not go) for the sake of diversity.

> LCS: So if you were—age appropriate, of course—but if you were to say, okay, "let's address white privilege, let's address patriarchy, let's address heteronormativity." If you moved beyond addressing inequality at the classroom level, just trying to get the kids to appreciate diversity, do you think you would get support from the parents, your principal, the district? In Lakeview?
>
> Ms. Parker: No. No. And it's funny because we [Ms. Parker and Ms. Roberts] started a parent conversation, um, last year under our former principal and Ms. Roberts and I had a kind of quick meeting with him [Mr. Brixton] like how can we push that forward.
>
> LCS: Push what forward?
>
> Ms. Parker: There was a big parent movement to have our dual language program ousted from the school.
>
> LCS: The parents didn't want it?
>
> Ms. Parker: Well, it was, "We don't have enough classrooms, and the class sizes in the gen ed are big and blah." Okay, granted all that is true, but when people ran the numbers that didn't change anything. The folks moving into the Morgan neighborhood is what's causing our building to be stretched to the seams. And, and they have a right to move in also, so it was on the district to provide a more appropriate space for us. But they [parents] didn't, they didn't want to go that route first. It was, "Let's get rid of those [Hispanic] families." And it really bothered me. Um, you know, and it bothered me for, all of that but also because they [nonwhite students] bring such a wonderful, something else to our building. So...
>
> LCS: And you and Ms. Roberts initiated the conversation?
>
> Ms. Parker: We, um, well, it, we had, um, we asked our principal to bring in the two ladies [from the anti-bias curriculum training program] to get this conversation started and, you know, very few parents came. It was really disappointing. And so when we said to him [Mr. Brixton] this year we'd like to continue that, his response was, "Well, they [parents] really feel beaten up about that." And it was like, really?!? So I don't feel like our parent population even wants to hear even just, "Let's embrace diversity."
>
> LCS: But dual language is still here at Morgan?
>
> Ms. Parker: Dual language is here. Well, the district is building. So the district is building an addition.

LCS: Has that quieted the talk of having dual language done away with?

Ms. Parker: It has. Yeah. It has for the time being. Um, but that would have been the second petition to oust the program, so—

LCS: When was the first?

Ms. Parker: Right after it [dual language program] came some parents started a petition, um, to get rid of it. I don't remember their reasoning at that point. I think that if I were to try to have those conversations in the classroom [about institutional discrimination], I don't really know what the parent reaction would be—

LCS: Yes, that's what I keep bumping up against as I talk to all the teachers. And living here myself. It seems so hypocritical to say we value diversity but we don't want those children at our school.

Ms. Parker: "We moved to Lakeview for the diversity. We love the brown children in my child's class!" But those are also the parents at this grade level that don't have those kids over for the play dates, don't invite those kids to the birthday parties because, "Well, they probably wouldn't be able to get there." First, how do you know that? And so you just don't invite them? I find that to be so offensive. And, I have a very hard time holding myself to parents sometimes, but I've had parents say to me, "Well, I see on your birthday chart that it's so-and-so's birthday [a racial minority child] and so I thought I would bring in a treat?" Why? You're assuming that that parent isn't going to? I feel like there's a judgment put on that parent.

In this conversation, Ms. Parker provides a number of examples that illustrate the disconnect between the social justice ethos of Lakeview and the everyday reality of living in Lakeview. While "Lakeview" is considered synonymous with "diversity," it is a brand of diversity that Woody Doane (2012) refers to as *color-blind diversity.* According to Doane:

In the decades since the Civil Rights Movement, it is increasingly socially desirable for individuals to embrace diversity in order to substantiate their non-racist or post-racial standpoint. Beyond the psychological benefits of feeling virtuous (most of us want to live in a society where race does not matter) "doing" diversity also provides individuals with a credential to use in racially challenging situations. (5)

As Ms. Parker points out, despite a stated commitment to diversity in District 21 and in Lakeview there has been more than one initiative to oust the dual language program at Morgan. (Most recently, the community considered a referendum to build a new school in an almost all-minority part of town that would encompass the Black and Hispanic neighborhood from which most of the minority students at Morgan are currently bused. While the initiative failed to receive the votes it needed to move forward, support for the new school was heavily encouraged at Morgan. As one teacher put it, "It was as if there was an implicit message that if we build this new school then you won't have to deal with *those* students in your school anymore.")

Further, Ms. Parker offers several firsthand accounts of the paternalistic attitudes among some of the white parents in her classroom when it comes to racial minority students. At times this occurs when parents situate themselves as benevolent white saviors as is the case in her example of the parents who offer to bring in treats when it is a student of color's birthday. At other times, it reveals itself when white parents choose not to invite minority children to extracurricular activities because they *know* it may be difficult for them to obtain transportation home. Given these experiences, it was not surprising that Ms. Parker did not believe discussing systems of oppression and privilege would be welcomed in her classroom or at Morgan.

On the other hand, Mr. Swain, a Black teacher at Mason, thought there might be some support for discussing institutional racism and sexism in District 21, but he was concerned about how these conversations would be received in Lakeview despite the town's commitment to social justice. Because Mr. Swain was originally from the South as was I, I asked if he thought there was less racism in Lakeview as opposed to the South, something a number of people whom I met in Lakeview assumed.

> No, it's, it's the same. And I think that's the thing you'll find. Or that I've found in Lakeview, too, or many places, I mean. I felt the same way about Texas. I think there you sort of know where people stand, but I think here it's a lot more subtle. And so you may not, um, people don't say how they feel and I prefer to know. (laughs) I like that about people in Texas because I knew where they stood. And I prefer people to be honest about what they think. I think here you do find that hypocrisy or just, just not being out front makes it harder to communicate those things, you know…you're not really sure what their motives, or what they're trying to get from it [initiatives to address institutional racism and sexism].

As Ms. Parker and Mr. Swain point out, Lakeview is a town known for its commitment to diversity and social justice. Yet, without the problematizing of unearned privilege and institutional racism and sexism, it is a commitment that ensures little more than superficial gains towards equality. Indeed, both Ms. Parker and Mr. Swain provide examples of behaviors that appear to reflect the frames of color-blind racism (Bonilla-Silva 2006) more than they do the tenets of antiracism. For example, Mr. Swain acknowledges the "more subtle" form of prejudice that occurs in Lakeview and questions the motives of some persons in the community who situate themselves as antiracists.

Paradoxically, it is Lakeview's reputation for social progressiveness I believe that shields many privileged residents from being forced to acknowledge the pervasiveness of racial and gender inequality. Living in Lakeview as a white person allows one to claim an identity marked by racial, gender, and sexual progressiveness, without necessarily having to confront and attend to racial, gender, and sexual inequality. This same phenomenon occurs when whites believe they can reject the label of racism and claim insider status on racial matters because they have a "Black friend" (Bonilla-Silva 2006), or straight people believe they can speak authoritatively about matters of homosexuality because they have a "gay friend": white residents of Lakeview need not prove their commitment to diversity, equity, and justice; they are residents of *Lakeview*, after all.

CONCLUSION

In the previous chapter, I illustrated how the organizational complexes (Smith 1990; 2005) in which the teachers participate reward them for following the rules, not rocking the boat. For example, while teachers continue to maintain some degree of autonomy, the structure of schooling in the district and in general is consistently moving towards the usurpation of teacher control over their own work: teachers are expected to utilize mandated curricula, implement best practice policy dictates, and submit to random surveillance, all while their career mobility is increasingly tied to student performance on standardized tests despite the diminishment or alleviation of teacher planning time and classroom supports. As a result, even if teachers *want* to address institutional discrimination and systems of privilege the organizational complexes in which they work make it improbable.

In this chapter, I introduced yet another obstacle that undermines the potential of teachers to serve as social justice advocates in the classroom: privilege. First, individual privilege associated with teachers' social locations can make it difficult for teachers to even recognize the pervasiveness of racism and sexism in schooling. As intersectionality theory warns (Crenshaw 1991; Bowleg 2008; Davis 2008), teachers' positions of privilege cannot be added or multiplied (e.g., Crenshaw 1991; Bowleg 2008; Davis 2008), however, the three white, straight male teachers I observed were the most resistant to acknowledging white privilege and male privilege. On the other hand, every teacher of color expressed concerns about racial inequality in schooling. There was not a similar parallel with regard to gender inequality; clearly, even most of the women teachers did not think that sexism was still a significant problem in schooling or society.

For those teachers, however, who were cognizant of enduring racism and sexism in schooling, privilege was still a mitigating factor in their reluctance to raise and address concerns about inequalities. Here, the main reason was that unearned privilege was simply not problematized. Teachers, administrators, and parents viewed privilege, particularly the influence of cultural capital (Bourdieu 1986) in the classroom, as a "good thing." Privileged (white) students reflected teachers' core beliefs in the proper family-school relationship (Lareau 1987; 2003), something that appeared to trump their concerns about the racial homogeneity of this group of students. Instead, the *problem* was disadvantage whether associated with race or poverty or both. In the end, as long as unearned privilege is understood to be inherently beneficial (McIntosh 1992), there is no space for teachers to critique systems of power like white privilege, patriarchy, heteronormativity, and ableism.

Further, while Lakeview has a reputation for being progressive, enlightened, and concerned with matters of social justice, the privilege associated with certain (white) residents also creates parameters around what are "acceptable" means to address race- and gender-related issues. For example, the brand of multiculturalism in District 21 that receives community support is not critical in nature, challenging systems of privilege and institutional discrimination, but a palatable way to attend to the needs and desires of students of color while increasing the "cultural competence" or cultural capital of white students (see also Darder and Torres 1998; Perry 2001; Lewis 2005). There are no in-school programs in place to attend to the needs and desires of girls, although based on the perspectives of most of the teachers in this study, this would be unnecessary since gender inequality is no longer a problem. In the end, the privilege associated with Lakeview, despite its ethos of social justice, can actually serve to mitigate the ability of the community to acknowledge white privilege, patriarchy, and heteronormativity, even while acknowledging the existence of inequality. This is a reality I am familiar with as a former white resident of Lakeview, and, indeed, throughout this project I was consistently confronted by my own privilege.

CONFRONTING MY OWN PRIVILEGE

I began this project critical of a number of issues including the pressure placed on children to compete and succeed. I fancied myself as the anti-helicopter parent who turned my nose up at *those* parents who enrolled their children in twenty different extracurriculars, feigned concern over the quality of every organic morsel their children placed in their mouths, and demanded their children receive all the enrichment opportunities in schooling they *deserved*. Yet, in many ways undertaking this research project served as a consistent and needed reminder of my own privilege.

Despite my overarching concerns about the new forms of tracking I observed in classrooms and the common wisdom that gender inequality was no longer a problem, I also found myself frustrated by the lack of time teachers' had available to challenge high-achieving students. Indeed, while there were demonstrable problems with a number of the strategies for attending to lower-achieving student needs, this was a mandated priority in District 21, especially given the reality of high-stakes testing. As a number of teachers in this study indicated in one fashion or another, pushing higher-achieving students to move to the next level was oftentimes not a priority given teachers time and human resource constraints. I was not the only person to raise this concern, as Ms. Stevens noted:

> Ms. Stevens: It's like the number one question I get from parents of these, you know, students who need enrichment. And I agree. They do need something, you know, further than what I'm able to teach them, and I, I mean we do work as hard as we can to like teach them how to do like peer coaching or I don't know. It's like, you know, we always tell the parents, "Oh, we're working on this. We're going to try this out." But I mean really, there's like no guarantee. I have written in my lesson plans meet with this enrichment group or meet with that enrichment group. But if I don't get to my lowest group, then like I'm sorry, but I just can't see the enrichment group today.

> LCS: And isn't it the case that you have to meet with lower-achieving students a certain amount of time each day?

> Ms. Stevens: Uh-huh. Like the kids who are reading below grade level, we have to see them either in a small group or one-on-one at least once a day, every day.

> LCS: So that demand has to be met regardless of whether you get to spend time with the higher-achieving students?

> Ms. Stevens: And I have nine students in here like that [RTI-Tier 2 students] so by the time I meet with nine kids whether it be in a group or independently, I mean my day is over, you know.

Even as this project drew to an end, I struggled with on the one hand wanting poor children, who were most often children of color, to have all the resources available to help them to be successful in school and in life, and on the other hand contemplating pulling my children out of District 21 schools despite our families' overwhelmingly positive experiences with my daughters' teachers. I did not want to be *that* white, educated parent who was advocating for more resources for her children despite the reality of living in a white supremacist society. Yet, there I was, spending practically every day in a classroom setting and not only seeing higher-achieving students often receive less one-on-one time with teachers but at times learning how to use their resources to navigate the classroom environment in order to appear as if they were working when they were really goofing off. Indeed, a basic tenet of differentiation is that children should be offered increasingly challenging ways to complete a task. Yet, when left to their own recognizances, students often choose the less taxing strategy so there is more time to do what they want to do, even if includes reading for pleasure.

In reality, District 21 does not have a "gifted" program. Students are supposed to receive various types of enrichment opportunities before, during, or after the school day that perhaps substitute in some ways for a comprehensive gifted program. Other enrichment opportunities are available on the caregiver's dime, leaving poor children at a disadvantage once again. Even so, a concern I found myself struggling with was the fact that lower-achieving students were often able to garner a larger proportion of teacher time and resources than those who were easily bored by the standard curricula because they were not being adequately challenged. Teachers often talked about the benefits of students learning from one another, but I was shocked by the lack of time some students actually spent interacting with their teacher during a typical school day.

While I supported the funneling of resources to struggling students and, indeed, highlighted in my research the shortcomings of current strategies for attending to these needs so they might hopefully be addressed in more effective ways, the lack of resources available for higher-achieving students was an issue that forced me to admit that perhaps I *was* one of *those* parents, wanting to know were my children receiving every resource they *deserved*. It is the same argument I find among my college students when I teach about inequality and privilege and the same argument Peggy McIntosh (1992) wrote about in her influential article on white privilege and male privilege: we are more willing to acknowledge inequality than privilege, and for those of us who acknowledge inequality, we generally want injustice to be addressed but do not necessarily want to give up our own unearned privilege in the process. This is but one example of the ways in which this project forced me to grapple with my own privilege, and while I continue to ask myself tough questions for which I do not always like my answers, asking these questions is my responsibility as a sociologist committed to feminist, antiracist goals.

Chapter Six

Confronting Paradox

In this book I have written a lot about paradox: paradoxes of education, paradoxes of race, paradoxes of gender. There is also something paradoxical that occurs in my own classroom when I teach courses on race. Inevitably, around the third week of the semester, undergraduates begin to ask why it is that only now—at eighteen, nineteen, twenty years of age—they are just learning about "all this." At three weeks in, "all this" usually refers to the social construction of race, the pervasiveness of white privilege, and intersectionality. This is an important question; and one that I use as a jumping off point to talk about the types of challenges I highlighted in the previous chapters.

However, when I begin to discuss the literature on race and education later in the semester, including my own research on color- and gender-blind classrooms, these same students will ask, "So what are you saying, Professor Stoll? Teachers should just tell eight-year-olds that because of their race, social class, gender, they have all these strikes against them?" 'Why didn't *our* teachers tell *us* about institutional discrimination and privilege?' becomes '*How* can we expect teachers to tell students about institutional discrimination and privilege?' This, too, is an important question, one reflective of students underlying concerns about whether teachers *should* address institutional racism and sexism, and if so, when and using what methods.

These are concerns I also wrestle with as I continue to think through the complexities of racial and gender inequality in schooling. Essentially, there are two distinct yet interrelated problems that must be addressed if we are to achieve equality in education. One problem demands that we address teachers' own biases and prejudices in the classroom. To do so requires us to formulate answers to questions such as: (1) how can we make teachers more aware of privilege and oppression? (2) How do we translate teachers' awareness of institutional racism and sexism into a desire for social justice advocacy? (3) How do we recruit and retain feminist, antiracist teachers?

The more pervasive problem that must be addressed however is an institutional one. Dominant group members have a vested interest in maintaining the illusion that we live in a post-racial and post-gendered society. In a meritocratic society like ours, the dominant narrative goes, one's potential is in no way limited by their race, gender, or any other group affiliation. In schooling, this logic is reflected in the *social equality maxim*: the decree that all students have the potential to be successful regardless of social location. Yet, racism and sexism remain persistent problems in schooling (Oakes 1985; Kozol 1991; Thorne 1993; Jenks and Phillips 1998; Bobbitt-Zeher 2007; Noguera 2008). How do educators account for these inequalities if they cannot take account of the material consequences of race and gender?

As I illustrated in chapters two and three, teachers often look to the frames of color-blind racism (Bonilla-Silva 2006) and gender-blind sexism to provide the answers. Yet, as I also argued, understanding how teachers think about race and gender and how they *do* both in the classroom are but one part of a larger story. Indeed, this institutional ethnography situates teachers within a complex web of interactions, a rigid hierarchy of authority, and bureaucratic policies and practices that reward them not for rocking the boat, but for following the rules—which includes constructing color- and gender-blind classrooms in order to realize the social equality maxim. This is particularly salient for those teachers who are not yet tenured.

To address inequality in schooling therefore requires us to take account of the *institutional* factors that undermine the potential for teachers to serve as social justice advocates in the classroom. As discussed in chapters four and five, these obstacles include the organizational complexes in which the teachers regularly participate and the countervailing forces of privilege. Without addressing these barriers to equality, teacher interventions are futile since these types of strategies only work to alleviate the *consequences* of institutional discrimination and only do so at an individual-level; putting teachers through "diversity training" may increase some teachers' "cultural sensitivities," but it cannot undo the racialized, patriarchal structure that provides the context for the everyday interactions that occur in their classrooms. Indeed, color- and gender-blind classrooms are by design structured to legitimate the ruling relations in place, not decenter them.

In this chapter I illustrate the link between these two fundamental problems—individual bias and structure—as I offer several insights about the teaching profession and educational policymaking that can hopefully get us one step closer to answering the fundamental question I raised in the first chapter: how do those of us concerned about social inequalities address issues of race and gender in schooling in an era of post-racial and post-gendered politics? I begin by challenging contemporary scholarship that views the lack of authentic caring on the part of teachers as the source of "the problem" and reconsider whether teachers should in fact be expected to serve as social justice advocates in the classroom. I then discuss the importance of including teachers in the conception and implementation of educational policy and offer a critique of No Child Left Behind. Finally, I offer considerations for future reform.

RECONSIDERING THE "CHALLENGE TO CARE"

I told a good friend of mine once, I said, "Teaching is more than just doing math, reading, science, whatever. Sometimes you're a mother, you're a nurse, you're a friend, you're everything to these kids. Everything. And if you can't see it that way, you're not going to do a good job because if the child is hungry, you don't teach him math or reading. He can't focus. He's hungry. You have something, you feed him, and then you teach him. You're building that relationship."

Ms. Martin, Second Grade General Education Teacher, Helis Elementary

Of the scholarship that has looked to the culpability of teachers in the perpetuation of inequalities in schooling, what has been particularly interesting is the argument that the inability of schools to provide a nurturing environment for their students (e.g., Noddings 1992; Harry and Klingner 2006) and the inability of teachers to "authentically care" (Valenzuela 1999) are to blame. According to Pedro Noguera (2008), for example, "There is no doubt that if schools were to become more nurturing and supportive, students would be more likely to perceive schools as a source of help and opportunity rather than an inhospitable place that one should seek to escape and actively avoid." (42) Noguera argues this is particularly important for the success of African American boys (see also Delpit 2006).

In 1992, Nel Noddings challenged, "The traditional organization of schooling is intellectually and morally inadequate for contemporary society. We live in an age troubled by social problems that force us to reconsider what we do in schools." (173) According to Noddings, the ultimate goal of education should not be to teach students how to read and write, but how to *care*. This, of course, challenges the common wisdom about the role teachers should play in the institution of education; indeed, according to Angela Valenzuela, "For the most part, teachers enter schools with the notion that their central preoccupation is to impart their expert knowledge. Layered over this expectation is a bureaucratically inefficient system that offers no incentives for prioritizing their students' welfare over 'the rules.'" (256) For teachers to *authentically care* for their students, according to Valenzuela, requires them to seek and develop connections with their students making trust the foundation for learning.

Of the race- and gender-related concerns I noted in this book, I do not believe the root of "the problem" is the lack of caring on the part of the teachers with whom I worked. In addition to observations in which teachers demonstrated a great deal of care for their students, I asked a number of questions in teacher interviews that revealed the extent to which *caring* as opposed to the ability to *teach* was understood to be the central function of the teacher. For example, when I asked teachers what qualities they possessed that they believed made them good teachers the responses included traits such as patience, dedication, empathy, understanding, and the love of children. Similarly, when I asked teachers if they could tell me about the qualities of an excellent teacher they had while growing up, teachers shared stories of a former teacher who stayed after school to work one-on-one with them, a teacher who did not give up on them even when they did not believe in themselves, a teacher who saw potential in them that had gone unnoticed by others. The general consensus was that excellent teachers were teachers who *cared*.

To argue that teachers fail to authentically care implies that caring for students is simply not valued as highly as teaching students basic curriculum, for example. However, when I asked teachers to tell me what they believed was the most important thing they did as teachers, rarely did someone mention teaching students how to read and do math, even though teachers' livelihoods were increasingly dependent on the ability of their students to master these skills. Instead, what the majority of teachers mentioned in one fashion or another was the importance of building relationships with their students.

Teachers also demonstrated care by their dedication to the profession. Despite the myriad demands placed on teachers in District 21, teachers willingly gave up free time in the summer to work on their classrooms and regularly brought work home at night and on the weekends because, as so many of them told me, they loved teaching. Indeed, inclusion co-teachers like Ms. Lee, as compared to regular classroom teachers, only have twenty minutes for lunch every day and no breaks when students are in fine arts, yet are not compensated any additional salary. Still, Ms. Lee told me that she would teach for free if necessary because she loved her job and dreaded retiring.

In conclusion, the teachers in this study clearly exhibited an ethic of care. As Mr. Gold told me, "Look, it's nice when they're [the students] learning, and they get high scores and so on, but that's not all of it." Therefore, in this institutional ethnography at least, the "problem" was *not* a lack of authentic caring as some scholars have suggested, but about the ways in which authentic caring is manifested—through the creation of color- and gender-blind classrooms that ultimately impede teachers' ability to attend to structural inequalities and systems of privilege. Teachers care for their students to the point perhaps they are afraid to address institutional racism and sexism for fear of how their students (and parents) will respond (e.g., Hooks and Miskovic 2011).

However, the organizational complexes of District 21 generally protect teachers from this potential anxiety by embracing multiculturalism and keeping teachers overextended with countless responsibilities and the specter of standardized testing. Indeed, the problem in District 21 is not a lack of caring, but a lack of time, in-depth knowledge about privilege and oppression, and an environment conducive to advocacy, that generally undermines teachers' ability to *care about* addressing institutional racism and sexism. These challenges along with the countervailing effects of privilege beg the question as to whether teachers are in fact ideally situated to serve as social justice advocates in the classroom.

LETTING TEACHERS OFF THE HOOK

While many social scientists including myself would like to see teachers serve as the conduits for social equality, this is not what the teachers in this study told me initially inspired them to pursue careers in teaching. In fact, while several teachers expressed a desire to help children overcome material hardships and a few wanted to work with populations of color in particular, not one teacher associated a career in teaching with dismantling institutional racism and sexism. This raises the fundamental question: can we expect teachers to devote their careers to social justice advocacy if this is not what they signed on for when they went into teaching?

Those who believe the answer to this question is yes, often look to teacher education programs as vehicles for training teachers to be more sensitive towards issues of racism, sexism, poverty, and heteronormativity (e.g., Aronowitz 2004; Delpit 2006; Abu El-Haj and Rubin 2009). However, when I asked teachers about courses they found particularly helpful once they entered the classroom as well as courses they found particularly useless, almost every teacher indicated what they remembered most about their teacher training programs came from coursework that provided opportunities for hands-on experiences in the classroom. In fact, a number of teachers told me if there was any problem with contemporary teacher education programs it was not the lack of training in cultural sensitivity for pre-service teachers but that pre-service teachers had to wait too long in their programs before entering the classroom to gain "real-world" experiences.

Interestingly, Stanley Aronowitz (2004) argues, "Teacher training should be embedded in general education, not in 'methods,' many of which are useless; instruction should include knowledge other than credential and bring the union/movement/organic intellectuals into the classroom." (33) Aronowitz assertion about the uselessness of methods courses, however, is contradicted by what the teachers in this study told me about the value of methods classes over general education coursework. Indeed, Mr. Foy indicated that the most beneficial classes were ones that taught pre-service teachers to organize and manage the classroom, including the basics of lesson planning.

In fact, when teachers did mention benefits they derived from non-methods classes such as Mr. Hamilton's educational philosophy and educational psychology classes or Mr. Gira's foundations of education class, it was generally considered beneficial because it helped pre-service teachers understand the basic underpinnings of contemporary pedagogical approaches, not serve as an impetus for social justice advocacy. Indeed, when asked about courses that helped teachers once they were in the classroom, no one mentioned classes they took that focused on race or gender with the exceptions of Ms. Parker who said she had drawn extensively on a class she took in multicultural children's literature and Ms. Smith who majored in inner-city studies and English as a Second Language. In fact, Ms. Smith was the only teacher in this study who told me that teacher training programs should focus more on teaching pre-service teachers how to respond to race- and gender-related needs in the classroom:

> LCS: Do you think this is missing by and large in teacher training programs today?

> Ms. Smith: Yeah. Yeah. Um, and those teachers who are identified as not being able to do that [work effectively with minority groups], need to get the training and then if they can't cut it, I'm sorry, but, you know, don't ruin generations of kids.

Despite the desire on the part of some scholars to have teacher training programs emphasize social justice advocacy (Valenzuela 1999; Delpit 2006), no teacher I worked with other than Ms. Smith indicated this was as important to pre-service teachers as methods courses, and, of course, hands-on training in the classroom. Further, as Felicia Parks and Janice Kennedy (2007) point out, exposing pre-service teachers to concepts such as institutional racism and sexism is not sufficient to ensure they will integrate a focus on social justice into their teaching philosophy; pre-service teachers must first recognize their own biases and seek to reduce them. Ms. Roberts and Ms. Parker learned this lesson firsthand when they sought to incorporate some of the strategies they acquired from their participation in the anti-bias curriculum series at Morgan.

Ms. Roberts and Ms. Parker voluntarily took part in the series for professional and personal reasons, as both are interracially married with biracial children. Because of their firsthand experiences with prejudice and discrimination, both teachers were receptive to addressing bias in the classroom including their own. Their colleagues, however, did not appear to be as receptive. In the following, Ms. Roberts explains what happened at Morgan when she tried to integrate some of the new techniques she learned in her anti-bias training.

> LCS: And so was the expectation that after the anti-bias training you would come back and try to implement it at Morgan?

> Ms. Roberts: We [Ms. Roberts and Ms. Parker] were working on it. We worked on it in our classrooms quite a bit and we also did some work at staff meetings. We invited the [anti-bias curriculum] facilitators to come to our school, the facilitators from the program...It's very, it was really very.... (sighs) It's a very good opportunity because it's something that can be put on the back burner, you know? And kind of also something that can be uncomfortable to talk about, so I think we [teachers in the program] all felt empowered every time we went to a session to keep it alive in our classrooms, the discussion about, you know, stereotypes, racism, you know all that—

> LCS: How was it received in the staff meeting?

> Ms. Roberts: Um...it was good (sounds skeptical). It wasn't enough, it's never enough is the problem.

> LCS: Do you think the other teachers were receptive, or...?

> Ms. Roberts: (pauses) For the most part, yeah. Yeah. But again it's one of those things like you have to make a conscious effort to keep it [anti-bias focus] alive.

When I asked Ms. Parker for her perception of how the staff at Morgan received the strategies for addressing bias in the classroom and in curricula, she was more cynical than Ms. Roberts:

> Ms. Parker: We were really encouraged [at the anti-bias training] to share with the staff [at Morgan]. She [Ms. Roberts] had the two [anti-bias curriculum] leaders come in and meet with our staff.

> LCS: How did that go?

> Ms. Parker: Um...hmmm... It felt like mixed reviews. I think teachers really do feel like their time outside of the classroom is precious, and I don't think anybody thought this isn't valuable, but—

> LCS: But maybe not on top of my priority list, or there are other things that . . .

> Ms. Parker: You know, the presenters were trying to give, like lay that foundational work, and I feel like people felt like 'we've heard all this,' you know...and so that was unfortunate I think.

In sum, based on their attitudes towards the benefits and scope of pre-service curricula and in-service teacher training, it appeared that most of the teachers in this study did not see their role as a teacher encompassing that of social justice advocate. While in the end there are certainly reasons to let teachers off the hook for not systematically addressing institutional racism and sexism, perhaps first and foremost because it is not the fundamental reason why most teachers go into the profession, there are important reasons to *not* let teachers off the hook. Despite education's role in perpetuating race- and gender-related inequalities, it is also an institution uniquely positioned to challenge these disparities, and teachers are therefore uniquely positioned to serve as social justice advocates.

In reality, no other institution monopolizes young people's lives to such a consistent degree from approximately age five through age eighteen. While teachers may want to avoid being on the hook for fear of guilt, shame, or retribution, being on the hook also means they are committed, obliged, and involved in addressing social inequalities in schooling (Johnson 2006). Indeed, there is potential for utilizing the institution of education to address systems of privilege and oppression, and because teachers are education's functionaries, it is imperative they remain on the hook when it comes to their role in perpetuating *and* alleviating institutional discrimination. If teachers remain on the hook, however, it is critical they are afforded much greater input in the development and implementation of educational policy than is currently the case.

ADDRESSING RACIAL AND GENDER INEQUALITY IN SCHOOLING

LCS: What do you think is the most pressing problem in education today?

Ms. Hurley: The increasing chasm of disconnect between those who make decisions about what we'll do and how we'll do it and, and the practitioners, the teachers.

Keeping teachers on the hook does not mean that we expect teachers alone to solve the problems of racism and sexism in schooling. Indeed, as I have already argued, this requires a restructuring of contemporary public education and society, a deliberate decentering of the post-racial and post-gendered politics that permeate our everyday lives. Keeping teachers on the hook at the most fundamental level reflects the recognition that teachers hold a unique position within the ruling relations (Smith 1990; 2005) of contemporary schooling as potential advocates for social justice-oriented policies that serve the interests of all their students. However, teachers cannot be expected to bear the responsibility of addressing racism and sexism in education if the disconnect that exists between those who make educational policy and the teachers goes unchallenged. Indeed, allowing teachers the space, legitimacy, and autonomy to address institutional discrimination and systems of privilege requires challenging the ruling relations and organizational complexes in which the teachers participate. Keeping teachers on the hook, therefore, means that we must allow teachers much greater input in shaping educational policy initiatives and in challenging reforms like No Child Left Behind and Race to the Top.

THE DISCONNECT

A common theme running throughout most of this book is the breakdown that exists between the theorization of educational policy and putting education policy into practice in the classroom. This breakdown often occurs because of the lack of influence teachers have over their own work. This, of course, is not a problem unique to District 21. As Mr. Swain, who works with the teachers' unions told me, it is a problem that extends well beyond the local level:

> You know, that's the thing, just the power base. Even the fact that legislation can pass that teachers aren't in favor of. Even with the national union, there was even one union that was sort of in favor of the, uh, Race to the Top, but, uh, the NEA [National Education Association] wasn't, um, a strong supporter of it. But, you know, these things pass anyway. Um, you know, with the votes in congress, even when you try to put pressure on them [politicians]. We didn't get the vote of confidence for, for the legislation but it, it still passes, you know.

I was also surprised to learn how removed administrators in District 21 and the school board were from everyday life in the classroom. Throughout my formal classroom observations from September through April, I never saw the superintendent or a member of the school board sitting in with classes. When I asked the teachers I worked with if the superintendent or school board members had ever come into their classrooms to observe what goes on, to see how educational policies look in practice, the answer was a resounding no. However, several teachers like Ms. Hurley welcomed the opportunity for administrators and board members to do so:

> I would love to see the superintendent and the board pick a teacher, a master teacher, somebody who's willing to form a partnership and then to make a commitment to spend several days a week in a classroom just to see what a teacher's life is like. I would, as I was saying earlier if I made a log of when I get up, and I brush my teeth, I mean, everything I do in my life, even the personal things, I watch TV, you know, I call two parents, whatever. If I made

a log I think they would be appalled to see that I don't have time to plan and to really use the data.

Witnessing the disconnect between the policymakers and the teachers in my observations served as the impetus for my decision to offer teachers some time in our final interview to talk about what they thought were the most critical problems currently in education given their unique experiences in the classroom every day. Interestingly, a number of the teachers talked about problems in public schooling that did not directly affect them, especially concerns about Chicago public schools including large class sizes and lack of curricular resources. Teachers also, however, shared concerns about other teachers in the profession. Mr. Hamilton, for example, described the biggest problem in schooling as the acceptance of failure related to the system of tenure, and told me that if students were not learning, then teachers needed to be fired.

Unfortunately, almost no one mentioned institutional racism and sexism when asked what they considered the most acute problems in education today. One exception was Ms. Parker who spoke passionately of her concerns about the plight of African American boys:

> I'm not sure if this is an educational problem but it's a societal problem for sure, and it sometimes keeps me up at night. Um, but we are failing our African American children. We're failing them, especially our boys. It just, you know, when you look at the, the percentage of young boys who drop out, who, who then turn to other things I… (tears well up in Ms. Parker's eyes) you know, it just is heartbreaking. Anyway, we, we went to a progressive educator conference, um, and Marian Wright Edelman gave the keynote and she talked very passionately about the cradle-to-prison pipeline and I thought, 'oh, my God! I'm a little chink in that pipeline!' It's awful! It's awful! And it bothers me to no end that when I look at my numbers, not necessarily how I've mixed my groups, but when I look at my numbers, my low kids are all my African American kids. Why?!? Why?!? And if I really keep everybody moving at a steady clip then they'll still be my lowest kids if everybody progresses. That is such a problem!

Interestingly, the purpose of the No Child Left Behind Act of 2001 (NCLB) was to address the vast inequalities in schooling to which Ms. Parker refers. Yet, in many ways NCLB is the prototypical example of the breakdown in educational policy and practice. Despite NCLB's stated intent, the policy itself and its implementation have resulted in numerous demonstrable pitfalls. As Nel Noddings pointed out in 2007, "Like so many reform movements, NCLB and its immediate predecessors started on the moral high ground—an expressed intention to close the achievement gap. But almost everything that followed by way of planning and implementation reveals a shocking level of moral obtuseness." (79) NCLB may have intended educational equality, but its sanctions were clearly underpinned by inequality. The teachers with whom I worked generally supported the legislation's goal of equity in education, but were quick to point out its many problems and the reasons it should be abandoned.

LESSONS LEARNED FROM NO CHILD LEFT BEHIND

When I asked the teachers I worked with for their feedback on NCLB, the responses were overwhelmingly negative. However, if there was any redeeming quality of NCLB, according to teachers, it was the legislation's emphasis on accountability. Teachers like Mr. Hamilton, for example, liked the mandates for empirical data attached to NCLB:

> Yeah, there's some very serious problems with what's expected [with NCLB], but some other things like, um, having honest, actual data that lets me know how my students are doing, making sure that, um, I'm responsible for my students and their learning, um, making sure that I'm aware of how students of different flavors are doing in my room, like I've got to know that. I have to know that, and I can't be using my psychic powers to find that out. You know, I've got to have some real, actual evidence, um, to support the kinds of things that I'm doing.

Overall, however, even teachers who work at Morgan, which consistently meets adequate yearly progress (AYP), had more criticisms than praise for NCLB. Indeed, some teachers like Ms. Hurley, believe NCLB has created a climate in schools that can deter potential teachers from entering the field:

> I can't imagine it being worse [than NCLB]. If I meet a young person who wants to be a teacher, I say, "Look, let's talk about what you're getting into." And when I see young teachers in the hallway and I go, "How are you doing?" and they go, "Overwhelmed." And they have tears in their eyes, you know. They say, "Has it always been this way?" And I go, "No, teaching used to be joyful!" It's not anymore most of the time. I have to create those moments and when I do I feel like I'm neglecting some responsibility somewhere, some paperwork, some, you know, pretest. You know, something that's being demanded of me that I can't possibly do and bring joy to learning.

Yet, perhaps the most pressing concern teachers mentioned was what they believed were the legislation's unrealistic expectations for student progress. According to NCLB, by 2014 all students are expected to be performing at grade level in reading and math. Mr. Foy is among several teachers I worked with who found this expectation ridiculous:

> Every kid, every child learns differently at a different pace, so to think that by—whatever it is—2012?—to think that every child is going to be reading at

grade level is completely—it's a ridiculous expectation to make! I think its politicians who are making education policy not educators.

Another major issue for teachers was the increased amount of testing in schooling that followed NCLB, especially the climate associated with high-stakes tests like the Illinois Standards Achievement Test (ISAT). This is a concern shared by a number of scholars as well (i.e., Aronowitz 2004; Duncan 2005; Noddings 2007). One consequence of the emphasis on testing is that it has forced teachers to focus on particular areas and to exclude others. According to Ms. Roberts:

> From the time that I started [teaching] kindergarten until now is just like, um, a tremendous change. Now, at our school we always, always, always had protected a block of time for play. Um, and I feel proud about that and I think that's important, but, um, you know, we didn't do guided reading. We didn't expect the kids [to know] how to read by the end of kindergarten. We didn't give reading tests. We didn't try to teach kids to work independently for big chunks of the day. So that's all changed and I would say kindergarten looks more like a first grade classroom did many years ago...That bleeds over into first grade, too, because I think that the young mind, and especially the need for them to develop vocabulary can't happen when their sitting by themselves, so it's just not how, how people learn words. I mean, you know, when you get old enough, yes, of course, you can because you have so many other things to attach meaning to, but so I mean the whole point of playing is that there's a, there's a reciprocal relationship going on with somebody, so...[not having time for play] concerns me.

There were also several teachers like Ms. Parker who were skeptical about the ability of standardized tests to accurately assess student growth:

> Um, I think that when we look at kids just based on the test score, just based on the ISAT or whatever standard of test we're giving them and when it's a very cut and dry, 'doesn't meet' or 'meets' or 'exceeds,' we don't take into account perhaps this child's growth. I mean, a child could come in and make more than a year's worth of growth and still 'not meet.' So that's problematic I think. And I think, um, it, it can turn some students off instead of saying, "Let's celebrate all this progress you've made!" Those tests don't tell you anything really about that child as a learner.

In addition, teachers lamented the amount of time they had to spend preparing students to take the ISAT, especially since it often came at the price of giving up time spent on other curricular areas. In my classroom observations, for example, science and social studies were always the subjects to get short shrift. In the following excerpt, Ms. Lopez discusses the consequences of the emphasis on testing.

What I believe is, um, what's happened since NCLB, um, is that I've had to focus more on testing, assessments where I didn't have to before. It was more making sure that the children learned, you know, it was a focus, you know, differentiating, enriching…but definitely what I've seen, how it's affected me here in this district is that, um, I've had to learn how to, uh, create spreadsheets. I've become a data expert. Um, [I] used to focus [on] integrating curriculum and working on, on all that, you know, and enriching my curriculum and making it fun and meaningful and learning and I think what it's done- I have less time to do that, um, a lot more time [spent] analyzing scores.

Similarly, while Ms. Chang did not believe teachers in the district were *teaching to* the ISAT, she told me that at Helis a good deal of time was required to teach the students *how* to take the test:

We do have to teach what the test is going to be like. I'm not teaching to the test, yet I know that I need to teach them the skills to pass the test because we know that the people who make up the test, they are, um, generally, white, um, men, women, you know, but they're from a different socioeconomic group then the children here [at Helis], and so therefore, um, we have to teach them the language, the format, and these children are also not as adaptable, I think, to subtle changes.

Finally, what I found particularly appalling about the effects of NCLB in the course of this research was the differential ways it affects teachers depending on the school where they work. For example, there is far more pressure placed on teachers at Mason and Helis to produce students who meet standards on the ISAT than at Morgan. This is not to say that teachers at Morgan do not work as hard or that they just coast through their day, however, because Morgan meets AYP every year, there is less stress associated with high-stakes testing for Morgan teachers. The teachers I worked with at Morgan like Mr. Hamilton and Mr. Gold, were far less likely to identify significant changes to their pedagogy as a result of NCLB, than teachers at Mason and Helis. Ms. Lopez, who taught at Helis before transferring to Morgan, offers an interesting perspective of the differences between the two learning environments:

Ms. Lopez: Well, it took, uh, it took a while to get used to it [teaching at Morgan]. I used to [teach at] Helis um, so, um, actually Helis was on academic warning the whole time I was there—

LCS: What does that mean?

Ms. Lopez: Not meeting annual yearly progress, academic warning. So we were, it was very strict and lots of requirements and, um, everything was looked at, um, with a fine tooth comb, you know, our, our assessments and this and that. And I came here [to Morgan] it was just kind of really laid back you know because this is a top-performing school.

LCS: So you don't feel that kind of pressure as much here at Morgan as you did at Helis?

Ms. Lopez: Yeah, but it was kind of, it was weird to come from that here.

LCS: Having worked in the two different environments what has made the difference in your opinion between Morgan as a top-performing school versus being on academic warning at Helis?

Ms. Lopez: Well, I think there's, um, several factors, you know. Um, I think it comes down to the, the poverty, you know. I think Helis has a higher, um, number of children of poverty and, um, that's what I see as [the] difference, you know. I see fabulous teachers in both schools, and both schools you know practicing best methodology, best practices, right? Um, but to be honest, I think here at Morgan we, we have a different population.

LCS: It seems like NCLB is much more of a concern for teachers who are at schools in the district that are not meeting AYP. Would you say that's true?

Ms. Lopez: Definitely. Definitely, it's a stressor…it's not fair.

LCS: Especially since your performance is tied to test scores, right?

Ms. Lopez: It's [test scores] tied to performance. It's tied to performance.

LCS: So it seems to me then that any teacher would be immediately at a disadvantage if they are working with a population of students who are struggling.

Ms. Lopez: Uh-huh. Poverty. It's about poverty. Uh, I had a teacher, um, who I will not identify but who was very upset because, um, he or she was getting a, um, new student who was way below grade level and it was going to effect the whole dynamics of the classroom. And so I, um, said, "Well, you know (laughs). You know, you can't have everybody, I mean, that's just life." And I was told that well, I signed up for this [to work with poor students]. I went into, uh, you know, bilingual. And, you know, this isn't about being bilingual or learning a second language. I'm dealing with poverty. So it's not because I deal with ESL. It's because there's such a high level of poverty.

Not only are teachers and students at Title I schools at a disadvantage when it comes to the ability to meet AYP, but they are also more likely to deal with language barriers as well since native Spanish speaking students also generally fail to meet standards on the ISAT. This is yet another strike against schools with a higher proportion of non-native English speakers as these students are required to take the ISAT in English, which according to Ms. Chang "anybody with a brain" should know does not make sense. There are in fact linguistically modified math and science versions of the ISAT, however, dual language teachers like Ms. Lopez told me they opt out of using these versions because if they do, they are not allowed to go over the test instructions with the students. In Ms. Lopez' experience, non-native English speaking students tend to do better when she can go over the instructions and repeat them if necessary. Interestingly, because of the Illinois state budget cuts this year the writing portion of the ISAT is not being administered in the lower grades. One consequence of this, however that Ms. Smith, a dual language teacher at Mason told me, is that some teachers are not teaching writing to their students.

Not only does administering the ISAT in English unduly affect the test scores of native Spanish speakers, but it also tends to compromise the mission of the dual language program. According to Ms. Lopez, "I think that's the hardest thing, how to help these children become bilingual, all of them, when I have such a demand to teach English and to prepare them for the test-you know for testing such as ISATs. I think they don't go together; it's like oil and water." Ms. Stevens, a dual language teacher at Helis, agreed:

> The state of Illinois has bilingual and dual language programs and they're not supporting those programs when they're giving, you know, all of the children the same exact [ISAT] test in English, expecting them to perform just as well as their monolingual peers. That's just not going to happen...I mean, it's not fair for the teachers, not fair for the principals because you know when we don't make—like, for example, we were just talking about the ISATs and how that test doesn't really measure the knowledge of some of our students because they're just not there yet. Well, we didn't make AYP because our bilingual subgroup didn't make progress where they were supposed to. So now we have all these things that are being mandated by the state that we need to do. The dual language teachers are like starting to, you know, prep the kids for the ISAT in English so that totally defeats the purpose of the dual language program for like two months because we're trying to prep these kids on how to take this test. And it is important that kids know how to take a test. I agree with that, like there's a whole genre of like learning how to, you know, take tests. That's important. That's just a life skill. On the other hand, they're in third grade. Like why do they need to be, you know, being prepped so hard for this test? And there's just so much pressure, you know, put on the kids and on the teachers.

While advocates of the No Child Left Behind Act of 2001 may have purported equality in education as their goal, as the teachers in this study make clear, the lessons learned since its implementation point to a number of significant shortcomings. Perhaps most far-reaching, NCLB ushered in an era of high-stakes testing that has changed the very structure of contemporary schooling with major implications for administrators, teachers, parents, and students. In his 2011 State of the Union Address, President Barack Obama indicated that NCLB would be replaced by another educational reform. What that reform will be remains to be seen, as does the amount of input that will be welcomed from teachers who are currently in the classroom. I do believe one thing is clear, however: unless we allow teachers greater input in the policymaking process, it is unlikely the current disconnect between policy and practice will be resolved in the foreseeable future.

CONCLUSION

In this book, I have attempted to weave together several important stories: one about teachers who care deeply about their students but are generally oblivious to the ways in which their words and behaviors reinforce dominant narratives about race and gender; one about dedicated, overworked teachers who are trying to keep their heads above water while meeting the myriad demands placed upon them in a climate of high-stakes testing; one about the disconnect between those who mandate educational policy and the teachers who are expected to implement these policies often with little or no input. Taken together, these stories provide the context for how racial and gender inequality in schooling operates in an era of post-racial and post-gendered politics. Indeed, mapping the ruling relations (Smith 1990; 2005), I believe, provides a rich understanding of how the organizational complexes in which the teachers participate intersect with the countervailing forces of individual and institutional privilege to mitigate their potential to serve as social justice advocates in the classroom.

In addition to the merits of employing institutional ethnography in this book, this research benefited immensely from the participation of a very diverse sample of teachers as well as from the selection of schools, the school district, and the town itself. First, because the teachers I worked with vary across several dimensions, this study offers a nuanced look into teachers' perspectives on race and gender. For example, the teachers in this study differ in the number of years they have taught, their age, race, gender, social class background, and sexual orientation (see Table 1.1). In addition, all three schools I worked at vary in the populations of students they serve (see Table 1.2 and Table 1.3). Morgan, a top-performing school is predominantly white, while Mason and Helis, both Title I schools, are predominantly Black and Hispanic, respectively. Finally, in this study I was also able to observe teachers *doing* gender and race (West and Zimmerman 1987; West and Fenstermaker 1995) in general education and dual language settings from kindergarten through fifth grade.

Also important to this research is the selection of diverse schools within the same school district. While a number of studies examining racism and sexism in schooling have included schools from different geographic locations within their sample (e.g., Thorne 1993; Lewis 2005), by working with schools with diverse student populations within a single school district I was able to control for a number of important variables frequently implicated in research on inequality in schooling, for example, class size, per pupil expenditure, and curricular resources (Kozol 1991). Indeed, despite having smaller average class sizes than Chicago Public Schools, particularly at Mason; despite a per pupil expenditure higher than the state average; and despite the presence of highly qualified teachers, all of whom in this study had at least one master's degree or a law degree, stark disparities continue to exist between the three schools, particularly with regard to the achievement gap. These disparities are in many ways related to factors beyond the control of individual teachers, such as students' prior skill sets before entering school, a variable clearly linked to poverty (e.g., Harris and Robinson 2007).

Further, this research benefitted from the selection of Lakeview as the setting for data collection. Lakeview is unique in several ways. It is racially diverse, politically liberal, residents have higher than average levels of formal education, and it is a town committed to an ethos of social justice. One might reasonably ask: if addressing institutional racism and sexism are not at the top of the priority list in Lakeview public schools, then where are they prioritized? If critical multiculturalism is absent in Lakeview, then where is it present? If gender inequality is not considered a problem in Lakeview, then where is it problematized? I believe the findings of this research concerning teachers' attitudes towards race and gender as well as their behaviors in the classroom are all the more compelling because they unfold in a town like Lakeview as opposed to a predominantly white, conservative suburb farther removed from the city of Chicago.

Finally, as a feminist, antiracist scholar, it is my desire to utilize my research in ways that hopefully advance progressive social change. As this project drew to a close, I found reasons to be skeptical that education could play a critical role in the alleviation of institutional racism and sexism, but also reasons to be hopeful. On the one hand, I think it is easy to dismiss the social justice potential in the current education system, especially since in order to systematically address racism and sexism requires changing more than one social institution. As Mr. Swain told me, "We tend to expect schools to fix all the problems of society, which it is not equipped to do."

David Tyack made this point in 1974 when he argued, "Urban schools did not create the injustices of American urban life, although they had a systematic part in perpetuating them. It is an old and idle hope to believe that better education alone can remedy them." (12) Three decades later, David Karen (2005) was still making the case that simply looking within schools to address social inequalities is futile since schools are but one part of what is essentially a societal problem:

> In thinking about why children perform differentially, we need to examine the larger patterns of resource distribution in the society: unequal access to medical and dental care; unequal access to housing; unequal access to labor markets and adequate incomes; unequal access to vibrant communities with high levels of social capital; and, yes, unequal access to educational resources. (168; see also Dworkin 2005)

Still, despite what may seem like overwhelming odds, there is a legacy within education that is essential in any quest for social justice (Tyack 1974: 11). I believe addressing inequalities in education is an important step in working towards progressive change in other social institutions. Revising a number of reforms at both the local and national level can serve as catalysts. Indeed, there are several incongruities associated with the NCLB legislation that demand attention before implementing new educational initiatives. For example, because NCLB measures equality in terms of test scores, equality is understood within a finite set of parameters. However, the definitions of equality teachers offer are far more nuanced:

> LCS: What does an equitable classroom look like to you? What does that concept, "equitable classroom," mean to you?

> Mr. Foy: I guess every child has equal access to the learning that's going on. They get the same materials, they get the same opportunities for learning that everyone else does. There's the same expectations for every, for every child, you know in spite of what kind of background they have, you have that same expectation. Um, but it means that you have to, you certainly have to adjust things for kids who struggle, to make it so that they can be successful. It might mean that equitable means that you make a change or an adjustment in what one child has to do because you know that for them to be successful the expectation has to be different than what [it might be for their classmate].

As this conversation with Mr. Foy illustrates, the teachers I worked with had fairly broad conceptions of equality, but for NCLB there is only one: AYP.

Further, NCLB by defining disparities in terms of test scores paradoxically establishes what types of inequalities are deemed important and which are not. Since test scores vary by racial group and by native and non-native English speakers in District 21, for example, racial inequality is problematized. However, because there do not appear to be the same stark differences with regard to gender in District 21, concerns about institutional sexism are practically nil. This begs the questions: (1) how should "equity" be defined; and (2) is standardized testing the best means to measure it?

In addition to macrolevel measures such as addressing the problems ushered in with NCLB, at the local level District 21 could benefit immensely by employing two full-time certified teachers in every classroom. After witnessing firsthand the breakdown in policy and practice, I am convinced there is no way to effectively carry out policies such as inclusion or differentiation without additional highly qualified staff. Further, with regards to hiring, I believe the recruitment of feminist, antiracist teachers can increase the probability of greater social justice advocacy in education than is currently the case. Non-critical multicultural add-ons that remain peripheral to the dominant Eurocentric curricula endemic to contemporary schooling, for example, do not seem nearly as efficacious for addressing individual *and* institutional racism and sexism as students interacting on a daily basis with educators who are committed to feminism and antiracism and structure the entire leaning environment to reflect this commitment.

Finally, in terms of addressing prejudicial attitudes, opportunities do exist to challenge teachers' common wisdom on race and gender given teacher mandates for professional development. This might actually prove to be more beneficial than focusing on teacher training programs where pre-service teachers are not able to immediately employ strategies for addressing race- and gender-related issues in the classrooms. However, as I have already argued, unless institutional changes are made, these interventions will ultimately fail.

In an era of "post-racial" and "post-gendered" politics the quest for social justice demands that we decenter the ruling relations in which the teachers participate by problematizing the adoption of the social equality maxim and the construction of color- and gender-blind classrooms. The color- and gender-blind classroom is built on the assumption-indeed, the stated maxim-that every student can learn and be successful regardless of social location. It is a learning environment that welcomes the celebration of diversity while denying the existence of institutional racism and sexism. How can teachers take account of the material consequences of race and gender if they cannot acknowledge they exist?

In the end, education is *not* a panacea for racism and sexism. However, I believe there is potential for social justice advocacy in education. To this the end, scholars must continue to both listen to and challenge teachers' perspectives on race and gender while recognizing that as long as the organizational complexes in which they participate are not problematized, the countervailing effects of privilege along with the increasing demands placed on teachers and their decreasing control over the profession are likely to impede any consistent efforts to address institutional racism and sexism.

Appendix A Initial Interview Instrument

INTITIAL INTERVIEW INSTRUMENT

Adapted from Lortie (1975)

PART I: Questions about Career Trajectory

- Q-1 Tell me about when you knew you wanted to be a teacher.
- Q-2 Thinking back to when you decided to become a teacher, what qualities did you feel that you possessed that would serve you well as a teacher?
- Q-3 Did you major in education as an undergraduate? If not, what field did you major in?
- Q-4 Tell me about any post-baccalaureate experience you have in education.
- Q-5 Thinking about your teacher training program, do you remember a favorite course or courses that you took? In what ways would you say this course(s) helped prepare you for the classroom?
- Q-6 Do you remember a course or courses that you liked least in your teacher training program? Did you find this particular course(s) not applicable to your classroom experience? How so?
- Q-7 How long have you been a teacher at this school?
- Q-8 What grade do you currently teach at this school? Have you taught other grades at this school?
- Q-9 Had you taught at a previous school or schools before coming to this school? If so, did you teach the same grade?
- Q-10 What attracted you to this school?

PART II: Questions about Teaching Pedagogy and Philosophy

- Q-11 What would you say is the most important thing that you do as a teacher?
- Q-12 What abilities or qualities would you say students need to possess in order to be successful in your class?
- Q-13 In your experience teaching, what would you say have been the most common obstacles that students who have not done well in your class have faced?
- Q-14 What is the greatest reward that you receive as a teacher? Why?
- Q-15 What is your greatest challenge as a teacher? Why?
- Q-16 What does an "equitable" classroom mean to you? Tell me about some of the things that you do to ensure there is equity in your classroom.

PART III: Demographic Questions

- Q-17 What is your current age?
- Q-18 Do you live in this community or do you have to commute? Where do you commute from?
- Q-19 Did your family live in this area of the United States while you were growing up?
- Q-20 What family members did you live with while growing up?
- Q-21 What was your father's primary occupation while you were growing up?
- Q-22 What was the highest level of education that your father completed?
- Q-23 What was your mother's primary occupation while you were growing up?
- Q-24 What was the highest level of education that your mother completed?
- Q-25 Are you currently in a long-term relationship? Are you married?
- Q-26 Do you have any sons or daughters? If so, are your children preschool age, elementary school age, middle school age, high school age, or college age?
- Q-27 What racial or ethnic group do you identify yourself as belonging to? Is this the same racial group that you would identify for your children?

Appendix B Final Interview Instrument

FINAL INTERVIEW INSTRUMENT

- Q-1 What effects of NCLB do you see in your classroom?
- Q-2 What is your overall opinion of NCLB? Benefits? Disadvantages?
- Q-3 What is your opinion of differentiated learning?
- Q-4 How do you do differentiated instruction in your classroom?
- Q-5 What strategies do you use to determine groups and partners?
- Q-6 What do you think are the benefits of differentiation?
- Q-7 What are the biggest challenges you have found with implementing differentiation?
- Q-8 What do you think about the district's inclusion policy?
- Q-9 What would you say are the benefits and disadvantages of inclusion for IEP students?
- Q-10 What would you say are the benefits and disadvantages of inclusion for non-IEP students in an inclusion classroom?
- Q-11 Historically, gender inequality has been a significant problem in schooling. Do you think gender inequality in schooling is still a major problem? Why not or how so?
- Q-12 Recently, some parents and educators have advocated for a return to single-sex public education, and NLCB made available 3 million dollars in grant money to experiment with such options. As a teacher, do you think this is a good way to address issues associated with gender in schooling? Why or why not?
- Q-13 Do you consider yourself a feminist teacher? Why or why not?

- Q-14 Historically, racial inequality has been a significant problem in schooling. Do you think racial inequality in schooling is still a major problem? Why not or how so?
- Q-15 How would you define an anti-racist teacher? Do you consider yourself an anti-racist teacher?
- Q-16 What do you think is the most pressing problem in education today?
- Q-17 Is this a problem at this school?
- Q-18 What do you think should be done to address it?

References

Abu El-Haj, Thea R. and Beth C. Rubin. 2009. "Realizing the Equity-Minded Aspirations of Detracking and Inclusion: Toward a Capacity-Oriented Framework for Teacher Education." *Curriculum Inquiry* 39: 435-463.

Ansalone, George and Frank A. Biafora. 2010. "Tracking in the Schools: Perceptions and Attitudes of Parents." *Race, Gender & Class,*17: 226-236, 238-240.

Archer, Louise, Anna Halsall, and Sumi Hollingworth. 2007. "Inner-City Femininities and Education: 'Race', Class, Gender and Schooling in Young Women's Lives." *Gender and Education* 19: 549-568.

Aronowitz, Stanley. 2004. "Against Schooling: Education and Social Class." *Social Text* 22: 13-35.

Artiles, Alfredo J., Nancy Harris-Murri, and Dalia Rostenberg. 2006. "Inclusion as Social Justice: Critical Notes on Discourses, Assumptions, and the Road Ahead." *Theory Into Practice* 45: 260-268.

Bem, Sandra L. 1993. *The Lenses of Gender: Transforming the Debate on Sexual Inequality.* New Haven: Yale University Press.

Benokraitis, Nijole V. and Joe R. Feagin. 1986. *Modern Sexism: Blatant, Subtle, and Covert Discrimination.* Englewood Cliffs, NJ: Prentice-Hall.

Berry, Ruth A. W. 2006. "Inclusion, Power, and Community. Teachers and Students Interpret the Language of Community in an Inclusion Classroom." *American Educational Research Journal* 43: 489-529.

Bettie, Julie. 2003. *Women Without Class: Girls, Race, and Identity.* Berkeley: University of California.

Blau, Judith R. 2003. *Race in the Schools: Perpetuating White Dominance?* Boulder, CO: Lynn Rienner Publishing.

Bobbitt-Zeher, Donna. 2007. "The Gender Income Gap and the Role of Education." *Sociology of Education* 80: 1-22.

Bobo, Lawrence D. 1999. "Prejudice as Group Position: Microfoundations of a Sociological Approach to Racism and Race Relations." *Journal of Social Issues* 55: 445-472.

Bonilla-Silva, Eduardo. 1997. "Rethinking Racism: Toward a Structural Interpretation."*American Sociological Review* 62: 465-480.

Bonilla-Silva, Eduardo. 2006. *Racism Without Racists: Color-blind Racism and the Persistence of Racial Inequality in the United States* (2nd ed). Lanham, MD: Rowan and Littlefield.

Bonilla-Silva, Eduardo and Gianpolo Baiocchi. 2008. "Anything but Racism." Pp. 137-151 in *White Logic, White Methods: Racism and Methodology*, edited by Tukufu Zuberi and Eduardo Bonilla-Silva. Lanham, MD: Rowman and Littlefield.

Bontempo, Daniel E. and Anthony R. D'Augelli. 2002. "Effects of At-School Victimization and Sexual Orientation on Lesbian, Gay, or Bisexual Youths' Health Risk Behavior." *Journal of Adolescent Health* 30: 364-374.

Bourdieu, Pierre. 1977. *Outline of a Theory of Practice.* Cambridge: Cambridge University Press.

Bourdieu, Pierre. 1986. "The Forms of Capital." Pp. 241-258 in *Handbook of Theory and Research for the Sociology of Education,* edited by John G. Richardson. New York: Greenwood Press.

Bowleg, Lisa. 2008. "When Black + Lesbian + Woman = Black Lesbian Woman: The Methodological Challenges of Qualitative and Quantitative Intersectionality Research." *Sex Roles* 59: 312-325.

Bowles, Samuel and Herbert Gintis (1976). "Beyond the Educational Frontier: The Great American Dream Freeze." Pp. 112-121 in *The Structure of Schooling: Readings in the Sociology of Education,* edited by Richard Arum and Irenee R. Beattie. Mountain View, CA: Mayfield Publishing Company.

Burke, Karen and Candra Sutherland. 2004. "Attitudes Toward Inclusion: Knowledge Versus Experience." *Education* 125: 163-172.

Bush, Melanie E. L. 2004. *Breaking the Code of Good Intentions: Everyday Forms of Whiteness.* Lanham, MD: Rowan and Littlefield.

Butler, Judith. 1990. *Gender Trouble: Feminism and the Subversion of Identity.* New York:Routledge.

Cahill, Betsy and Eve Adams. 1997. "An Exploratory Study of Early Childhood Teachers' Attitudes Toward Gender Roles." *Sex Roles* 36: 517-529.

Campbell, Marie and Frances Gregor. 2004. *Mapping Social Relations: A Primer in Doing Institutional Ethnography.* Lanham, MD: AltaMira Press.

Campbell, Patricia B. and Ellen Wahl. (1998) 2002. "What's Sex got to Do With It? Simplistic Questions, Complex Answers." Pp. 722-733 in *The Jossey-Bass Reader on Gender in Education,* edited by Elisa Rassen. San Francisco: John Wiley & Sons, Inc.

Carbonaro, William J. 1998. "A Little Help from My Friends Parents: Intergenerational Closure and Educational Outcomes." *Sociology of Education* 71: 295-313.

Carr, Meghan K. 2007. "Single-Sex Education." *The Georgetown Journal of Gender and the Law* 8: 483-503.

Chapman, Thandeka. 2008. "Desegregation and Multicultural Education: Teachers Embracing and Manipulating Reforms." *Urban Review* 40: 42-63.

Colander, David and Jessica Holmes. 2007. "Gender and Graduate Economics Education in the U.S." *Feminist Economics* 13: 93-116.

Cole, Elizabeth R. and Safiya Omari. 2003. "Race, Class and the Dilemmas of Upward Mobility for African Americans." *Journal of Social Issues* 59: 785-802.

Coleman, James S. and Thomas Hoffer. 1987. *Public and Private High Schools: The Impact of Communities.* New York: Basic Books.

Collins, Patricia H. 2000. *Black Feminist Thought: Knowledge, Consciousness, and the Politics of Empowerment* (2nd ed). New York: Routledge.

Collins, Patricia H. 2008. "Reply to Commentaries: Black Sexual Politics Revisited." *Studies in Gender and Sexuality* 9: 68-85.

Collins, Randall. 1979. *The Credential Society: An Historical Sociology of Education and Stratification.* New York: Academic Press.

Connell, Robert W. 1987. *Gender and Power.* Stanford: Stanford University Press.

Crenshaw, Kimberle W. 1991. "Mapping the Margins: Intersectionality, Identity Politics, and Violence Against Women of Color." *Stanford Law Review* 43: 1241-1299.

Crosnoe, Robert, Catherine Riegle-Crumb, and Chandra Muller. 2007. "Gender, Self-Perception, and Academic Problems in High School." *Social Problems* 54: 118-138.

Darder, Antonia and Rodolfo D. Torres. 1998. "Social Theory and the 'Race' Fixation: A Critique of Multicultural Education Discourse." *Cultural Circles* 2: 17-32.

Davis, James A., Tom W. Smith, and Peter V. Marsden. 2002. *General Social Surveys, 1972-2008.* Chicago, IL: National Opinion Research Center.

Davis, Kathy. 2008. "Intersectionality as Buzzword: A Sociology of Science Perspective on What Makes a Feminist Theory Successful." *Feminist Theory* 9: 67-85.

Delpit, Lisa. 2006. *Other People's Children: Cultural Conflict in the Classroom* (2nd ed). New York: The New Press.

DeVault, Marjorie L. 2006. "What is Institutional Ethnography?" *Social Problems* 53: 294-298.

Doane, Ashley W. 2012. "Shades of Color Blindness: Rethinking Racial Ideology in the United States." Presented at the Annual Meeting of the Southern Sociological Society, New Orleans, Louisiana, March 22-25, 2012.

Douglas, Susan J. and Meredith W. Michaels. 2004. *The Idealization of Motherhood and How It Has Undermined All Women.* New York: Free Press.

Du Bois, W. E. B. 1903. *Souls of Black Folks.* New York: Penguin Books.

Duggan, Lisa. 2002. *The New Homonormativity: The Sexual Politics of Neoliberalism.* Durham, NC: Duke University Press.

Dumais, Susan A. 2002. "Cultural Capital, Gender, and School Success: The Role of Habitus." *Sociology of Education* 75: 44-68.

Duncan, Garrett A. 2005. "Critical Race Ethnography in Education: Narrative, Inequality and the Problem of Epistomology." *Race Ethnicity & Education* 8: 93-114.

Dworkin, A. Gary. 2005. "The No Child Left Behind Act: Accountability, High-Stakes Testing, and Roles for Sociologists." *Sociology of Education* 78: 170-174.

Entwisle, Doris R., Karl L. Alexander, and Linda Steffel Olson. 1997. *Children, Schools, and Inequality.* Boulder, CO: Westview Press.

Farkas, George. 1996. *Human Capital or Cultural Capital? Ethnicity and Poverty Groups in an Urban School District.* New York: Aldine Transaction.

Feagin, Joe R. 2006. *Systemic Racism: A Theory of Oppression.* Routledge: New York.

Ferguson, Ann A. 2001. *Bad Boys: Public Schools in the Making of Black Masculinity.* Ann Arbor, MI: The University of Michigan Press.

Foster, Michele. 1990. "The Politics of Race: Through the Eyes of African-American Teachers." *Journal of Education* 172: 123-141.

Gutmann, Amy. 1987. *Democratic Education.* Princeton, NJ: Princeton University Press.

Hardaway, Cecily R. and Vonnie C. McLoyd. 2008. "Escaping Poverty and Securing Middle Class Status: How Race and Socioeconomic Status Shape Mobility Prospects for African Americans During the Transition to Adulthood." *Journal of Youth and Adolescence* 38:242-256.

Harris, Angel L. and Keith Robinson. 2007. "Schooling Behaviors or Prior Skills? A Cautionary Tale of Omitted Variable Bias within Oppositional Culture Theory." *Sociology of Education* 80: 139-157.

Harry, Beth and Janette Klingner. 2006. *Why Are So Many Minority Students in Special Education? Understanding Race & Disability in Schools.* New York: Teachers College.

Holstein, James A. 2006. "Institutional Ethnography." *Social Problems* 53: 293.

Hooks, Debra S. and Maja Miskovic. 2011. "Race and Racial Ideology in Classrooms Through Teachers' and Students' Voices." *Race Ethnicity and Education,* 14: 191-207.

Hurtado, Aida. 1996. *The Color of Privilege: Three Blasphemies on Race and Feminism.* Ann Arbor, MI: University of Michigan Press.

Idol, Lorna. 2006. "Toward Inclusion of Special Education Students in General Eduction: A Program Evaluation of Eight Schools." *Remedial and Special Education* 27: 77-94.

Ingersoll, Richard M. 2005. "The Problem of Underqualified Teachers: A Sociological Perspective." *Sociology of Education* 78: 175-178.

Jencks, Christopher and Meredith Phillips. 1998. "The Black-White Test Score Gap: An Introduction." Pp. 1-51in *The Black-White Test Score Gap* edited by Christopher Jenks and Meredith Phillips. Washington, D.C.: Brookings Institution Press.

Johnson, Allan G. 2006. *Privilege, Power, and Difference* (2nd ed). New York: McGraw-Hill.

Johnson, Allan G. 2005. *The Gender Knot: Unraveling our Patriarchal Legacy* (2nd ed). Philadelphia: Temple University Press.

Kane, Emily W. and Elsie K. Kyyro. 2001. "For Whom Does Education Enlighten? Race, Gender, Education, and Beliefs about Social Inequality." *Gender & Society* 15: 710-733.

Karen, David. 2005. "No Child Left Behind? Sociology Ignored!" *Sociology of Education* 78: 165-169.

Kozol, Jonathan. 1991. *Savage Inequalities: Children in America's Schools.* New York: HarperPerennial.

Kozol, Jonathan. 2005. *The Shame of the Nation: The Restoration of Apartheid Schooling in America.* New York: Three Rivers Press.

Lareau, Annette. 1987. "Social Class Differences in Family-School Relationships: The Importance of Cultural Capital." *Sociology of Education* 60: 73-85.

Lareau, Annette. 2003. *Unequal Childhoods: Class, Race, and Family Life.* Berkeley: University of California Press.

Lasser, Jon and Deborah Tharinger. 2003. "Visibility Management in School and Beyond: A Qualitative Study of Gay, Lesbian, Bisexual Youth." *Journal of Adolescence* 26: 233-244.

Lent, Sandra A. and Josefina Figueira-McDonough. 2002. "Gender and Poverty: Self-Esteem Among Elementary School Children." *Journal of Children & Poverty* 8: 5-22.

Lewis, Amanda E. 2004. "What Group? Studying Whites and Whiteness in the Era of Color-Blindness." *Sociological Theory* 22: 623-646.

Lewis, Amanda E. 2005. *Race in the Schoolyard: Negotiating the Color Line in Classrooms and Communities.* New Brunswick, NJ: Rutgers University Press.

Lindsay, Jo, Amaryll Perlesz, Rhonda Brown, Ruth McNair, David de Vaus and Marian Pitts. 2006. "Stigma or Respect: Lesbian-Parented Families Negotiating School Settings." *Sociology* 40: 1059-1077.

Lipsitz, George. 2006. *The Possessive Investment in Whiteness: How White People Profit from Identity Politics.* Philadelphia: Temple University Press.

Lorber, Judith. 1994. *Paradoxes of Gender.* New Haven, CT: Yale University Press.

Lortie, Dan C. 1975. *Schoolteacher: A Sociological Study.* Chicago: The University of Chicago Press.

Marx, Sherry and Larry L. Larson. 2012. "Taking Off the Color-Blind Glasses: Recognizing and Supporting Latina/o Students in a Predominantly White School." *Educational Administration Quarterly,* 48: 259-303.

McIntosh, Peggy. 1992. "White Privilege and Male Privilege: A Personal Account of Coming to See Correspondences Through Work in in Women's Studies." Pp. 70-81 in *Race, Class, and Gender: An Anthology,* edited by Margaret L. Anderson and Patricia Hill Collins. Belmont, CA: Wadsworth Publishing Company.

McNeil, Michelle. 2008. "Single-Sex Schooling Gets New Showcase." *Education Week* 27: 20-21.

Mills. 1997. *The Racial Contract.* Ithaca, NY: Cornell University Press.

Newkirk, Thomas (2000) 2002. "Misreading Masculinity: Speculations on the Great Gender Gap in Writing." Pp. 314-328 in *The Jossey-Bass Reader on Gender in Education,* edited by Elisa Rassen. San Francisco: John Wiley & Sons, Inc.

Noddings, Nel. 1992. *The Challenge to Care in Schools: An Alternative Approach to Education.* New York: Teachers College Press.

Noddings, Nel. 2007. *When School Reform Goes Wrong.* New York: Teachers College Press.

Noguera, Pedro A. 2008. *The Trouble with Black Boys: And Other Reflections on Race, Equity, and the Future of Public Education.* San Francisco: Jossey-Bass.

Oakes, Jeannie. 1985. *Keeping Track: How Schools Structure Inequality.* New Haven, CT: Yale University Press.

Okopny, Cara. 2008. "Why Jimmy Isn't Failing: The Myth of the Boy Crisis." *Feminist Teacher* 18: 216-228.

Omi, Michael and Howard Winant. 1994. *Racial Formation in the United States: From the 1960s to the 1990s.* (2nd ed.) New York: Routledge.

Orr, Amy J. 2003. "Black-White Differences in Achievement: The Importance of Wealth." *Sociology of Education* 76: 281-304.

Parks, Felicia R. and Janice H. Kennedy. 2007. "The Impact of Race, Physical Attractiveness,and Gender on Education Majors' and Teachers' Perceptions of Student Competence." *Journal of Black Studies* 37: 936-943.

Pascoe, Cherie J. 2007. *'Dude, You're a Fag': Masculinity and Sexuality in High School.* Berkeley, CA: University of California Press.

Perry, Pamela. 2001. "White Means Never Having to Say you're Ethnic: White Youth and the Construction of 'Cultureless' Identities." *Journal of Contemporary Ethnography* 30: 56-91.

Pollock, Mica. 2008. *Everyday Antiracism: Getting Real about Race in School.* New York: The New Press.

Risman, Barbara. 1999. *Gender Vertigo: American Families in Transition.* New Haven, CT: Yale University Press.

Rivers, Caryl and Rosalind C. Barnett. 2006. "The Myth of the 'Boy Crisis.'" *The Washington Post.* April 9. Retrieved June 30, 2009. (http://www.washingtonpost.com/wp- dyn/content/article/2006/04/07/AR2006040702025.html).

Rothman, Barbara K. 1989. *Recreating Motherhood.* New Brunswick, NJ: Rutgers University Press.

Saunders, Jeanne, Larry Davis, Trina Williams and James Herbert Williams. 2004. "Gender Differences in Self-Perceptions and Academic Outcomes: A Study of African American High School Students." *Journal of Youth and Adolescence* 33: 81-90.

Sax, Leonard. 2005. *Why Gender Matters: What Parents and Teachers Need to Know About the Emerging Science of Sex Differences.* New York: Three Rivers Press.

Siperstein, Gary N., Robin C. Parker, Jennifer N. Bardon, and Keith F. Widaman. 2007. "A National Study of Youth Attitudes Toward the Inclusion of Students with Intellectual Disabilities." *Exceptional Children* 73: 435-455.

Sleeter, Christine E. 2012. "Confronting the Marginalization of Culturally Responsive Pedagogy." *Urban Education,* 47: 562-584.

Smith, Dorothy E. 1990. *The Conceptual Practices of Power: A Feminist Sociology of Knowledge.* Toronto: University of Toronto Press.

Smith, Dorothy E. 2005. *Institutional Ethnography: A Sociology for People.* Lanham, MD: AltaMira Press.

Smith, George W. 1998. "The Ideology of 'Fag': The School Experience of Gay Students." *The Sociological Quarterly* 39: 309-335.

Solomon, R. Patrick, John P. Portelli, Beverly-Jean Daniel, and Arlene Campbell. 2005. "The Discourse of Denial: How White Teacher Candidates Construct Race, Racism and 'White Privilege.' *Race Ethnicity and Education,* 8:147-169.

Sommers, Christina H. (2000) 2002. "Why Johnny Can't, Like, Read and Write." Pp. 700-721 in *The Jossey-Bass Reader on Gender in Education,* edited by Elisa Rassen. San Francisco: John Wiley & Sons, Inc.

Sorokin, Pitirim. 1959. "Mechanism of Social Testing, Selection, and Distribution of Individuals within Different Social Strata." Pp. 182-212 in *Social and Cultural Mobility.* Glencoe, IL: Free Press.

Sprague, Joey. 2005. *Feminist Methodologies for Critical Researchers: Bridging Differences.* Walnut Creek, CA: AltaMira Press.

Stromquist, Nelly P. 2012. "The Educational Experience of Hispanic Immigrants in the United States: Integration through Marginalization." *Race Ethnicity and Education,* 15: 195-221.

Stryker, Susan. 2008. "Transgender History, Homonormativity, and Disciplinarity." *Radical History Review* 100, 145-157.

Suter, Jesse C. and Michael F. Giangreco. 2009. "Numbers that Count: Exploring Special Education and Paraprofessional Service Delivery in Inclusion-Oriented Schools." *The Journal of Special Education* 43: 81-93.

Tarrant, Shira. 2006. *When Sex Became Gender.* New York: Routledge.

Theoharis, George and Marcelle Haddix. 2011. "Undermining Racism and a Whiteness Ideology: White Principals Living a Commitment to Equitable and Excellent Schools." *Urban Education,* 46: 1332-1351.

Thorne, Barrie. 1993. *Gender Play: Girls and Boys in School.* New Brunswick, NJ: Rutgers University Press.

Thurlow, Crispin. 2001. "Naming the 'Outsider Within': Homophobic Pejoratives and the Verbal Abuse of Lesbian, Gay and Bisexual High-School Pupils." *Journal of Adolescence* 24: 25-38.

Tomlinson, Carol Ann. 2000. "Reconcilable Differences? Standards-Based Teaching and Differentiation." *Educational Leadership* 58: 6-11.

Tomlinson, Carol Ann. 2004. "The Mobius Effect: Addressing Learner Variance in Schools." *Journal of Learning Disabilities* 37: 516-524.

Tomlinson, Carol Ann and M. Layne Kalbfleisch. 1998. "Teach Me, Teach My Brain: A Call for Differentiated Classrooms." *Educational Leadership* 56: 52-55.

Tong, Rosemarie P. 1998. *Feminist Thought* (2nd ed). Boulder, CO: Westview Press.

Tyack, David B. 1974. *The One Best System: A History of American Urban Education.* Cambridge, MA: Harvard University Press.

Valenzuela, Angela. 1999. *Subtractive Schooling: U.S.-Mexican Youth and the Politics of Caring.* Albany, NY: State University of New York Press.

Vera, Hernon and Andrew Gordon. 2003. *Screen Saviors: Hollywood Fictions of Whiteness.* Lanham, MD: Rowman and Littlefield.

Volonino, Victoria and Naomi Zigmond. 2007. "Promoting Research-Based Practices Through Inclusion?" *Theory Into Practice* 46: 291-300.

Walby, Kevin, 2005. "How Closed-circuit Television Surveillance Organizes the Social: An Institutional Ethnography." *The Canadian Journal of Sociology* 30: 189-214.

Walby, Kevin. 2007. "On the Social Relations of Research: A Critical Assessment of Institutional Ethnography." *Qualitative Inquiry* 13: 1008-1030.

Weber, Max. 1946. "The 'Rationalization' of Education and Training." Pp. 240-244 in *From Max Weber: Essays in Sociology,* translated by H. H. Gerth and C. Wright Mills. Great Britain: Routledge.

West, Candace and Sarah Fenstermaker. 1995. "Doing Difference." *Gender & Society* 9: 8-37.

West, Candance and Don Zimmerman. 1987. "Doing Gender." *Gender & Society* 1: 125-151.

Williams, Katya, Fiona Jamieson, and Sumi Hollingworth. 2008. "'He was a Bit of a Delicate Thing': White Middle-Class Boys, Gender, School Choice and Parental Anxiety." *Gender and Education* 20: 399-408.

Wilson, William J. 1978. *The Declining Significance of Race: Blacks and Changing American Institutions.* Chicago: The University of Chicago Press.

Yosso, Tara J. 2002. "Toward a Critical Race Curriculum." *Equity & Excellence in Education,* 35: 93-107.

Index